CONFESS
URBAN I
WILDLIFE (
WASHINGTON STATE

Washington Fish & Wildlife
Officer Greg Haw, w-160 (retired)

ISBN- 978-1-6707-93515

Some names have been changed. The contents are factual as the author recalls but subject to the fallibilities of human memory. Interpretations of the law contained within are the author's opinion only. They are not to be considered legal advice.

Cover photo- The 60-year old author taking a break between loading up poacher's nets full of McAllister Creek chum salmon

Contents

Forward

July 1st, 2019

Immediately after retirement in June of 2019 I went into a slight depression. I was no longer one of the boys. My police commission was cancelled, I turned in all my gear and I faced the rest of my life for the first time without a job.

While in slight depression, I realized that nearly all economically valuable populations of fish as well as much of our native flora and fauna are in a sorry state. Native animals are being squeezed out by non-native and invasive species that the government has introduced and that they protect. Recreational hunting and fishing opportunities are shrinking, shrinking, shrinking.

Each day produces environmental news stories reflecting gross inaccuracies that the public accepts as the gospel truth. These falsehoods are furthered by malicious politicians who exploit these myths for political gain. An almost biological cycle of ignorance has taken over, and similar to influenza…it's contagious.

An alarming amount of eco damage has occurred on my watch! Is it possible that after dedicating 39 years protecting the natural resources of Washington State, at times taking significant risks, I contributed nothing?

I started making a few notes of my 39-year career. Almost instantly a compulsion to keep writing took over. I have almost no idea of what I am going to say. Some may find it interesting. Here goes.

The Birth of a Fish Cop

Somehow, I graduated from the police academy in June of 1986. As a brand new Fish Cop I assumed a residence in the town of Forks Washington. A rather depressing little place at the time. Logging still dominated the local economy but anyone could see that things were changing. The hot button "Eco" issue of the day involved spotted owls. Their protection under the Endangered Species Act had greatly limited the harvest of local timber. Jobs were being lost. Local attitudes were very much anti-government, so much so that state employees, particularly those of the Department of Natural Resources (A significant local employer), found it nearly impossible to rent or purchase homes. A popular bumper sticker of the day, clearly an attempt to antagonize environmentalists stated *"Earth First, we'll log the rest later."*

As the new fish cop in town I had little trouble finding a place to live. This was largely due to the fact that as a bachelor, I was not burdened with having to please a spouse. My new home was a rundown double wide trailer near the Sol Duc River on the outskirts of town. I had many furry roommates.

Forks was still the Wild West as far as the rest of the state was concerned. Getting punched in the jaw did not necessarily involve the police and drunk drivers were often merely driven home by local cops. There were lots of tough guy types and heavy drinkers. Two notorious drinking establishments were situated across Main Street from one another. Brawls often spilled out of one and into the other. In one case I was told that a man threatened another with a gun. He was quickly disarmed but the gun fired shooting off the victims thumb. The "victim" while bleeding, assumed control of the gun and perused the "assailant" across the street and shot him in the head at the front door of the other joint. I recall seeing the blood on the sidewalk. The death was considered "Justifiable" the only punishment being that the shooter was deported. Often, when I read about sanctuary states, I wonder if he ever came back.

4

Another famous story, one that was still fresh as I arrived in town allegedly involved the outlaw motorcycle club "Hells Angels". (Although the locals would not have differentiated between outlaw groups.) The bikers, according to the story took over the town during a 4th of July celebration. The current chief of police told me the outlaws were acting up and causing trouble. The Chief ordered them out of town, the order was refused. He incorporated the use of the town's one and only fire truck and "washed them off the street." The bikers left, never to return.

The "West End", as we called it boasted the best steelhead fishing in the world at the time and local rivers held salmon nine months out of the year. Saltwater salmon and ground fish fishing was world famous with small boat fishing dominating the action. Commercial fishing was a big deal at three local ports. It seemed like the Olympic National Park was everywhere one looked.

Best of all as far as I was concerned, were the many un-gated logging roads which offered this rookie fish cop unlimited daily adventures. It was truly a great place to be.

***

The one advantage that I had in regards to assimilating into this new job was that as an angler, I had a good understanding of recreational fishing regulations. I had an uncommon knowledge of fish and fishing and a well-rounded general wildlife knowledge base. Otherwise I was woefully unprepared for nearly all aspects of the job. I had never even got a ticket, let alone seen one issued. I had never before even stepped into a police car other than into burnt out training cruisers at the State Patrol driving course.

My brother was a Washington State trooper, he had sparked in me an interest in law enforcement. Because of my relative youth, family connections and quite frankly a little dumb luck I was able to pass a series of tests and a background check. Now, to my amazement I was driving a fully equipped police unit, with all the lights and sirens. I did not have the foggiest idea of how and when to turn them on. (That was not taught at the academy.) I resembled a police officer because of the official markings and uniform but I had no business patrolling on my own.

***

During my first week on the job I drove around familiarizing myself with my new beat. LaPush and the lower Hoh River, Sekiu, Neah Bay, all the while waiting for someone to tell me what to do. It took a week or so to have a phone installed. I carried a role of quarters for the public phones that were still in use. I did not want to be a pest to my boss, so I just waited for direction which was slow in coming. I was finally contacted by my sergeant. He drove out to Forks, his childhood home. Together we drove around the area and talked about fishing. I recall that late in the day I explained that I only had in my possession four bullets for my revolver. (Target ammo from the academy.) My new boss gave me six real bullets. Feeling a little better (although I still had no spare rounds) I still felt half naked like in a bad dream. Thankfully he provided me with a list of fellow detachment officers. The nearest one, a guy that I vaguely knew, lived about sixty miles away. Win Miller became my first mentor.

I had maintained contact with one of my academy buddies who had been assigned to the Grays Harbor patrol area. The ocean salmon fishery was in full swing and he excitedly reported that he had written many tickets and was having all kinds of adventures under the mentorship of a veteran officer. I felt left behind and at the same time challenged. Tomorrow is the day…I'm going to write some citations. Wisely I first called the neighboring officer and asked a few questions that must have sounded ignorant. How much is the fine for undersize chinook? Unlawful gear? Over limit? Which of the carbon copies do I hand the violator? What do I do if the guy won't sign the ticket? My questions went on and on. I took notes. My

6

plans went off without a hitch and I recall writing several tickets for undersized chinook in Sekiu. I quite arbitrarily chose a fine amount of $25. (I soon learned that the correct fine was $95.)

Slowly but steadily I became competent with routine recreational fishing patrols. I remained incompetent with all other aspects of the job including filing the tickets with the local court. I recall the local judge, now a Justice on the Washington State Supreme Court, laughing when she saw me submitting tickets. I had carefully separated all of the carbon copies from one another along the perforated line thinking I was being helpful to the court clerk. The reality being that she then had to reattach them all with scotch tape. A task taking 30 minutes.

I soon discovered that the Quillaute River System, consisting of the Quillaute, Calawah and Sol Duc Rivers held summer chinook and sockeye salmon starting in early summer. Salmon fishing remained closed yet schools of fish were observable in all of the slow deep holes especially, for some reason, those associated with bridges. It was therefore easy to incorporate these potential hot spots into a variable patrol rout. In all of these locations telltale trails, discarded fishing paraphernalia and the occasional splash of blood on the rocks were indications, even to the dumbest fish cop, of unlawful fishing. It was at this point that I started to feel like I could do some good for the world.

***

Salmon snagging is a crime although due to well-meaning but ignorant regulators its definition has been muddied due to misguided attempts to fix a law that was not broken (1). It is defined as an act of angling where the fish does not take the bait or lure voluntarily in its mouth but is instead intentionally impaled on a hook while "minding its own business." It's more like gaffing a fish, no angling skill is required, and it's very wasteful with a high mortality factor for fish that get away (even higher mortality for those that don't). Even habitual snaggers hate other snaggers and often report their competitors to the fish cop. The act is associated with a violent sweeping motion of a fishing rod and large single or treble hooks weighted from below.

There was one notorious location on the Sol Duc River locally referred to as the "Bark Hole." (2) During low summer flows Chinook salmon would hold here and essentially remain until fall rains prompted them to swim upstream to spawn. Aware of the unlawful nature of their actions, local snagger's would often employ counter surveillance tactics. Due to the high bank overlooking the hole, it was easy for posted lookouts to warn others of the fish cops approach which was almost always by vehicle. What I had going for me was the fact that the highly visible fish were often too tempting for the lookout who would inevitably get bored and join in on the fun.

It was here, in my 27th year of life that I began to understand the virtues of patience. I also learned that the sound of gravel popping under the weight of truck tires carried a great distance. I developed a tactic accordingly. I would sneak in on foot, watch them snag and retain a fish, recover the fish and gear. Easier said than done! Any veteran officer would have done it much differently. He or she would have simply called in a partner and each would park at either end of the access trail. They then would have simply caught the violators red handed in possession of the closed season fish as they went home, and used the inevitable snag injuries to support the criminal charge of snagging. Also, only a fool of a poacher would have recorded the catch on a record card which would have prompted yet another charge. I would learn these things over time.

(1) All popular salmon streams have their own "Bark Hole". They go by many names. To me it will always be a fishing hole dominated by snagger's and unlawful anglers.

(2) Now The term "Flossing" describes the unlawful attempt to "Snag" a fish in the mouth when the fish does not take the bait or lure but is hooked "on or about the head." Ironically, due directly to the "Anti Snagging Rules", Snagging", is far more difficult to enforce than it once was.

Over the course of the summer and fall of 1986 and for many subsequent years my salary meant almost nothing to me. I took few days off and often patrolled 12 or more hours per day. I thought nothing of suiting up and heading off to work three times in a 24 hour period. When I needed an unmarked car I used my own. I became obsessed and must have been a bore to my friends and family because all I could talk about was work. In those days officers scheduled themselves largely based on unofficial patrol priorities. We were "officially" limited to working no more or less than 171 hours per month. I ignored this directive due to my obsession and a sympathetic lieutenant, who strangely enough seemed to appreciate the work I was doing. It was not uncommon for me to log 240 plus hours of work per month. I later learned that this obsession for work was common for new officers. The job was so much fun that going fishing, something that I had always loved to do, was a letdown and boring by comparison. I was not paid for the extra hours nor did I expect pay. I once filled the gas tank of my patrol car at the Clallam Bay Mobile Station before learning that they did not accept the state issued credit card. I thought nothing of using my own card and never requested reimbursement. Was this dedication or stupidity? A little of both I think.

***

I need to explain that at this point in time there were fish cops and there were game wardens. Two "Gamies" were stationed in Forks with me. Both were very helpful and seemed almost too interested in improving my skills. They worked for a different state agency and had different authorities, background and training requirements. I for example had been hired with the first group of fish cops where a certification from the Washington State Criminal Justice Training Academy was a requirement of employment. Game wardens, often referred to

9

as gopher chokers, greenie meanies or mallard marshals, had no such requirement and didn't till much later. Fisheries patrol officers also carried federal commissions because we often patrolled outside waters, beyond state lines. Fish cops and gamies often patrolled the same streams, they on one side working steelhead and trout, with us on our side working the far more abundant salmon. (3) They focused on hunters in the fall while we patrolled salmon spawning streams. (This was a ridiculous set up and was rectified by legislative action later.) We all got along well enough but after the two agencies merged years later, some jealousies did develop. Few officers remain that worked through this period. The conflicts are largely forgotten.

(3) Both sides had their kooks, deadwood and malcontents. Both also had rising stars that would go on to do amazing things.

***

Most of the memories of my maiden year in Forks are very clear. The chronology of events however is blurred.

I recall walking the Sol Duc River and hearing brush breaking nearby. While investigating the strange noise I found a fresh silver bright sockeye salmon on the ground. (My recollection of the condition of the fish suggests mid-July at the latest.) Then I found another and another. To my utter amazement a man that I was unaware of stepped out of the brush carrying a stringer of the 3 pound fish. He said "You got me, I give". I did my best to pretend that I had seen him snag all 27 of the sockeye and requested that he retrieve his rod and reel that I was pretty sure he had stashed. The man complied. He went home with numerous criminal citations and no fish. I recall donating these beautiful fish to the Clearwater work camp. It took absolutely no skill to make this pinch. It was dumb luck on my part and very bad luck for the violator. Were I not totally obsessed with patrolling, this memorable pinch never would have been made. I could not sleep at night, thinking this kind of activity was going on behind my back.

***

Just above tidewater on the Quillaute I approached a man and his son fishing from a drift boat. They were anchored along the bank under some overhanging alder trees. Close enough to hear them talking, it became clear to me that the dad was teaching his kid how to snag salmon, and it was a school day to boot! I crept close and saw them snag and retain several coho. At times I was splashed by the fish as they were being landed, all without being seen. As the dad made a back cast in another attempt to snag a fish I reached out and impulsively grabbed his leader and simulated a fish like tug on the line. The man, thinking that he had hooked a fish on his back cast let out a whoop. He looked back and saw me holding his snagging gear. The man, clearly embarrassed, said nothing and handed me his identification. He must have thought I was a ghost, the most sneaky fish cop ever! Again it was just dumb luck on my end. I had no desire to humiliate him so I calmly issue a ticket and seized the fish. I promised myself that I would not tell this tale to any of the locals for fear of further embarrassing the violator. A twisted version of the story soon circulated around town. The word on the mean streets of Forks was that I had planted snagging gear on the violating dad, made the kid cry and stole the fish. Of course the defendant never brought these exculpable allegations before the judge but the damage to my reputation was done. If this would have happened to me later in my career I would have laughed out loud. At this point I took it personally. Soon, another version of the story went viral around Forks. This one alleged that the dad shit his pants when surprised by the officer and that's what made the kid cry... I was very immature at the time.

***

So far things were going well and my confidence was improving each day. I was still working mostly alone and had not yet felt threatened physically. There were a very few threats to kick my ass and a false story that someone had thrown me off the dock at LaPush but nothing serious. One day this changed. It was now early October and the run of coho and fall chinook were staged up in tide water on the Quileute River. The tribal gillnet season was set to open this night. Although fisheries biologists were concerned for the inevitable slaughter due to extremely low water, the tribal fishing right trumped the state's authority to impose a closure. The fishery was a go.

Earlier in the day I had encountered a man and cited him for a run of the mill crab violation at a place called East Twin River. The man was difficult but without much trouble and with the assistance of the only West End State Trooper whom I had befriended, I processed the violation. While wrapping it up and releasing the man from cuffs he stated that he was a tribal member and his Indian buddies were going to take care of me in a violent way. This man may have had some Native American blood but I knew that he did not have treaty fishing rights. I chuckled as he told me he was from Oklahoma and visiting for the summer. I had encountered him numerous times on the lower river sometimes with a fish tote (commercial fishing paraphernalia) in his truck. I suspected at the time that he may try to unlawfully engage in the tribal fishery. This suspicion was later confirmed to me by a tribal fisheries officer.

Putting two and two together, I made plans to watch the off reservation tribal fishery expecting this man to take part. I know now that if this guy would have been seen gillnetting the river by lawful native fisher he would have been "dealt with" and not in a pleasant way. I know for almost certain that the tribal fishers would <u>not</u> have reported it to the white fish cop, but some form of justice would be done. Recklessly, I decided to walk in to the fishing area after dark with a Viet Nam era surplus "starlight scope." This particular unit was only marginally useful but it gave me comfort because I was at the time, and remain, uneasy in the dark.

12

The route to the fishing area would take me about ½ mile across a sometimes flooded river bottom adjacent to the Olympic National Park boundary. I recall being completely ignorant of the jurisdictional issues. I was aware that I would have to cross property owned by a well-established local family whose loyalties I had not bothered to look into.

Around midnight I was feeling my way along and listening for the river. While still disoriented I heard "Hey You". I looked behind me and illuminated a spot with my flashlight. I saw a man, whom I recognized, sitting under a bush pointing a shotgun at me. At one point the barrel touched my belly. It's funny what one remembers under stress but I distinctly recall that the gun was a 16 gauge Browning semi auto. I remember the smell of beer and that this was the man that I had seen many times buying his daily case of beer (a 24 pack) at the Three Rivers Store. I was too stupid to be scared right then. I said, "Put the gun down Lenny, I'll leave if you want me to."

I recently found my notes for October 11, 1987 that document this contact. I had not seen these notes for over 32 years. The reader of this needs to be aware that my current recollection of what happened appears to be distorted. I wonder now if my notes at the time were a distortion. I'll never know. They read precisely as follows:

23:50 hours Contacted subject at Richwine Road with shotgun directed at me demanding me to leave his property he then laughed and said he was hunting game wardens (drinking)? He later became amiable but would not give his name. Advise F-19 by phone.

I walked off in the direction that I came. I remember thinking that if he would have shot me he could have easily argued justification. After all it was I that was armed and trespassing at night on his property. My fear grew after the danger had passed. This was a very strange feeling. I remember reaching for the door handle of my patrol car to keep from falling. I was very frightened. I don't recall telling this story

13

before, I have always prevented myself from thinking about it. I have heard from a reliable source that "Lenny" no longer drinks and is doing well 34 years later. This past summer 2019, I patrolled Forks one last time and half heartily looked for Lenny. The "scene of the crime" was unrecognizable to me. Associated homes had disappeared, apparently in a flood that happened thirty years prior. It was as if the event did not happen. I did not find Lenny, maybe that was best.

Eye witness testimony is perhaps the worst form of evidence. It is fallible and subject to a multitude of factors, not the least of which is the passage of time and stress. Give me a bloody glove any day, I don't even care if it still fits!

***

I firmly believe that if a police officer isn't getting "beefed" occasionally he or she is probably not doing their job. Complaints are inevitable, the likelihood increases based on the volume of contacts. (Ambiguous and unnecessary regulations and poor management don't help.) I also believe that if an officer gets three or more minor citizen complaints in say a 6 month period, he or she, and their supervisor should probably reevaluate the officer's approach to people. There were times when I deserved a complaint, not because I did anything unlawful, but because my initial approach was not soft enough. I learned over time to engage the average person socially first, then to ease into a full blown compliance check.

All citizen complaints are taken seriously by management. All are followed up with an interview. I learned to anticipate the complaints. I would dutifully call my boss and tell him what I may have done wrong and what to expect. I often submitted a written report on incidents where I expected a complaint which was never made. This gave me much needed credibility with supervisors and came in very handy later on. A large percentage of complaints were outright falsehoods here is an example:

A father wrote to my lieutenant that I had entered Forks High School and jerked his son out of class. I had allegedly interrogated him somewhere on campus and got him to confess to a fishing crime that he did not commit. My lieutenant seemed to believe this story. He called me and conducted an interview. I told him that I had done no such thing but I may be able to shed some light on the subject if I knew the man's name. I vaguely recognized the name and racked my memory. The prior weekend, I had contacted his son on the lower Sol Duc. This is what really happened and exactly what I reported:

I observed a group of kids (16 year olds) who were actively snagging visible coho just upstream of the Lyndecker Bridge. One of the kids had climbed a tree and was directing the other two where to cast. In this manner several closed season coho were hooked but all came off. I decided to break this snagging party up before any fish were killed because I was not willing to cite these youngsters. I made contact, chewed them out a little and asked to see their licenses. (A $3 Personal Use Fishing License was required at the time.) One of the kids, the complainant's son, did not have the required license. I warned all the kids and let them go after I gave the one kid a $5 bill and directed him to walk to Three Rivers Resort and buy a license. He agreed to do so. There was no expectation regarding repayment.

Later that same evening I returned to the scene of the crime and observed the same three kids engaged in salmon snagging. This time they had killed numerous fish. They had carefully removed the valuable bait roe from the female fish so the complainant (A licensed guide) could take paying customers fishing. This time I issued each a citation for salmon snagging. ($365 fine) Then I asked to see the complainant's sons fishing license. The boy only produced a pack of cigarettes and some change. The contact ended at the river bank and I had never been inside Forks High School, I explained. Clearly the complainant's son felt compelled to tell his dad this whopper in order to justify the loss of the bait!

My lieutenant later told me that he had interviewed the father and given him my account. When dad heard the part about me giving the kid money for a license but instead bought cigarettes he snapped. He suddenly terminated the interview and withdrew his complaint. I heard later that the kid did not go fishing for a year and may have received a fat lip. The dad never apologized to me but always treated me well after that.

***

I wrote earlier about a father and son snagging incident, the one where I grabbed the dads snagging gear on his back cast. This contact also generated a barely recognizable written complaint, signed by dad but written in a woman's hand. The letter demanded my immediate termination. Again I had to explain that I did not plant the snagging gear in the boat nor did I did steal the fish. I was a little nervous because I had no evidence of my innocence other than my statement. I was exonerated. I later learned that the woman who wrote the letter did so while coerced by her abusive and illiterate husband. One year later, this same woman came to my home and reported that her husband and son were regularly fishing with "DuPont Spinners" (dynamite fishing.) Concerned that her son would be blown to bits she requested my help in getting sole custody of the son. I declined, not sure which parent was the best choice.

Supervisors understand that if a complainant is upset about merely about getting a ticket, there's not much to look into. If it's a bad case, due process of law will exonerate the defendant. The bottom line is usually "Why didn't the officer just give me a warning?" When a violator asks, Are you going to write me a ticket?" often a direct answer of "yes" is the best approach. Many people find this answer arrogant and rude. This alone sometimes sparks a complaint.

***

The Crow brothers lived in broken down old logging camp near the source of Lake Creek. Ranging in age from about 14 to 20 they lived with their mother. (4) Lake Creek provided spawning habitat for a large portion of the late fall run of huge chinook inhabiting the Quillaute system. These fish were so big that snagger's had a hard time landing them on conventional tackle. (I saw numerous fish over 50 pounds and at least two over 60.) Their size protected them from snagger's somewhat in the main river, but after entering the confines of Lake Creek they became more vulnerable. The Crow's considered Lake Creek their own. All were incorrigible snagger's. One I convicted in a trial for "stoning" spawning chinook. There were numerous snagging arrests as well. Another time I encountered the brothers walking on a trail with the most impressive catch of beautiful spring chinook that I have ever seen. They were carrying the fish like porters for a big game hunter, all were skewered on a stiff pole cut just for this purpose. The season was "open" and the limit was two each. They were experienced violators and knew better than to submit to any questioning. The totality of the circumstances as well as their obvious smirk as they passed by convinced me that I had been beat again. It still haunts me.

(4) *I often saw this worn out woman paying her sons fines at the local courthouse which she, judging by her appearance, could ill afford.*

***

I often found stashed gaff hooks along the banks of Lake Creek and several times removed "rag nets." (Small sections of gill net with large mesh.) I discovered places, associated with this gear, where carcasses were scattered. These dead fish at first sight resembled naturally spawned out carcasses but upon inspection I soon realized that they were all female fish. These fish were often slit from vent to gills with only their eggs removed. A possible connection emerged. A local school teacher was marketing a product called "Johnson Sandwiches" which were sold locally at tackle shops. These extra-large salmon eggs, single eggs processed and sold in jars, were a popular local trout bait. I made some enquiries and learned that this school teacher processed this product at home using a family recipe, and shopped them around town. I did my best to conduct an investigation but without experience working such issues my attempts failed. I interviewed the teacher and a tackle shop owner and confirmed many of my suspicions but I was "Over my head" and failed to put together a chargeable case. An article appeared in the local weekly paper describing how I had harassed the shop owner and seized some of this product. This was not true and I confronted the man, a paraplegic confined to a wheelchair after suffering a logging accident. His response was "Sorry Greg, I sell more reels when people feel sorry for me." I lost a great deal of respect for this man as a result, and for the local newspaper, but I walked away with a much better understanding of small town dynamics.

***

I was responsible for conducting boat patrols from essentially La push on the outer coast, around Cape Flattery and the western half of Juan de Fuca Straights. We had a 23 foot Glasply on a trailer, a smaller aluminum boat or two as well as a 43 foot "Delta" complete with modern electronics and a very fast rubber boat that could be launched off the deck. Boat patrols were fun and we wrote many citations to unsuspecting violators who were inevitably very surprised by our sudden appearance coming out of a fog bank. It was not uncommon to write twenty or more citations in a day but I admit that since I was willing to do the associated work that other, more experienced officers, were quick to pass off their tickets to me. I later learned later that they still claimed credit for a pinch but I would be responsible for all follow-up. I was happy to do it.

In contrast to dock work, boat patrols often caught anglers by surprise, often while still in the act of hiding overages, undersized and unlawful species. This is where I first heard the term "Fillet and release", which means when translated, the act of removing an unlawful fish's flesh, hiding same and discarding the carcasses overboard. Often, after doing so with large Yelloweye rockfish, a species of great concern, the carcasses would float on the surface due to an extended air bladder. After spotting such a fish, commonly one could patrol up-drift and find another and another. Sometimes this trail of bread crumbs would lead directly to the violating vessel. A little simple questioning combined with a reasonable search would invariably result in the seizure of a cooler full of contraband. The story that would be spread around port was that over aggressive "Water Nazis" were randomly searching boats and taking lawful rockfish fillets. I even heard a version of this story on a local outdoor radio program. I took every opportunity to correct these stories with the facts ...short of calling the radio station. I never got over having my integrity questioned. It bothers me to this day.

***

In those days fish cops were generally unsupervised and were trusted with incredible freedom to patrol as they wished. Rarely was this freedom taken advantage of. Once while working the Canadian line off Sekiu, we made an exception. My partner and I developed an interest in the shoreline of Vancouver Island. (A whole different country as Forrest Gump would say.) I recall a wonderful day most of the time spent with a lone gray whale following the kelp line. We found ourselves entering Victoria Harbor. What the hell, we tied up to the customs dock and requested permission to look around. It was granted, the only condition being leaving our pistols aboard the patrol boat. Dressed like what may have looked like Canadian sailors, we had lunch wearing white t-shirts and gray uniform pants. I recall writing citations in U.S. waters on the return trip.

Another time we took a similar liberty and actually risked getting into serious trouble. A friend of mine smuggled aboard the patrol boat a medium weight mooching rod with a 3 ounce dart jig or two. He was an avid angler and his justification was that since this was an overnight trip we were entitled to food. "What was better?" he argued, "The state paying all of us each $30 per day in meal money or we could save the tax payers the expense by fending for ourselves!" As the new guy I went along and ultimately played an active role.

We were somewhere in the San Juan Islands at a location named Shark Point. The patrol boat was positioned so that the aft end was not in the line of sight of nosey waterfront home owners. Soon one rod was deployed and it seemed only an instant before a fish was hooked. It became clear that the fish was not the target species, a lingcod, but instead a Chinook salmon of about 20 pounds. With no dip net or gaff on board, and due to my experience as a hatchery man who bragged to have tailed many thousands of Chinook, I was tasked with grabbing the fish. While standing on the swim step and grabbing the rail with one hand the fish was easily landed. I assure the reader that the season was OPEN and that lawful gear was used. The only violation being that we did not eat the fish for dinner and pocketed the meal money.

***

At first I always issued verbal warnings for most of the violations I considered minor such as, fail to record catch and barbed hooks. I justified this decision by understanding that at the time these violations were criminal by definition. To be more specific, these acts were classified as gross misdemeanors. This means that a person convicted of such a thing could conceivably go to jail for a year. At this point in my career I felt that educating the public about these regulations would eventually lead to improved compliance. I however never observed improved compliance by employing this enforcement tactic. What ultimately became obvious to me was that the third day of a three day weekend, after writing a bunch of tickets during the first two, compliance always greatly improved! Conclusion: Warnings usually don't work, they just reinforce the unlawful behavior. They do however greatly reduce the frequency of citizen complaints.

One day our lieutenant drove up and met with my detachment. It was more of a social event thinly disguised as a "Detachment Meeting." One work related topic came up however. It was mid-September. In Sekiu the coho fishing remained great but most anglers had left for the season. The Lt. stated that he had been contacted by a Washington Department of Fisheries statistician. This "bean counter" as he was referred too, had come across some suspicious numbers. The term "negative catch bias" came up, none of us knew what that was. In a very primitive way it was described like this:

"The fish counters are seeing more limits of fish at the docks than they are seeing angler trips."

This could mean only one thing, there was a lot of two tripping going on!

Two tripping simply means that an angler goes fishing, returns with his daily limit and immediately goes back out for a second limit. The data was suggesting that even three tripping was rampant. This phenomenon is symptomatic of good fishing and a lack of enforcement presence. Other members of the detachment took this as an insult to their efforts. My peers cried bullshit! Being a fish counter in a prior life I believed the bullshit!

Without consulting my supervisor or crew I got up early the next morning (a scheduled day off) I set up at Van Ripers Resort, because it afforded the best view of retuning boats and a place to hide my car. By seven a.m. a boat with three persons returned with nine coho and went back out. (In those days the daily limit was three salmon per angler.) This scene was repeated to the point that I was forced to limit my observations to only six boats because quite frankly that's all I could keep track of. If I was going to make cases I had to separate each and every violating boat and document each offload in great detail.

These six boat boats were the tip of an iceberg, I had to stay focused. All six, and no doubt many others, returned to the dock with extra limits. I filed charges on all of the occupants of the violating boats and felt good about my efforts. I received no positive feedback from my peers or supervisors, it's likely that it made them look bad, I'm not sure. I remember being chastised by one partner for donating the fish to the local prison. He felt they should have gone to the Clallam Bay elders. He was probably right about that.

Many years later I was approached by a very bookish looking man at headquarters in Olympia. He introduced himself and said that he wanted to thank me. "For what", I asked? He explained that he was a statistician for the Department of Revenue and that while working for the Department of Fisheries he noticed the disturbing catch trends at Sekiu 15 years prior. He thanked me first of all for believing him at the time. He added that my efforts had proven his mathematical theory. "How had you heard about the cases I made?" I asked. He told me that I had busted one of his neighbors.

***

Were it not for a very unwise decision that I made after my second year in Forks, I may have finished my career there. Tragically, and beyond all reason I decided to marry the court clerk. During daylight hours she was very good looking but prior to each morning's application of 5 pounds of makeup, unrecognizable. (Not in a good way.) An unnecessary courthouse wedding resulted in my decision to move to the Seattle duty station for the sake of the marriage. I must have been insane to have made this decision. At this point in my life I can't think of a place where I would rather not be. (If I could go back in time I would find myself and say "run you dumb bastard, run like hell.") We were soon settled in the worst possible part of Kent Washington.

Surprisingly the work was great. I had my own patrol boat moored at Shillshole Marina. The city itself provided unlimited opportunity to patrol shore bound anglers. Salmon snagging was rampant on the Cedar River as well as on the Duwamish. Commercial fishing, brokering and retail fish markets were everywhere. If I wished, I could patrol anywhere I wanted in King, Kitsap, Snohomish or even east to adjacent eastern Washington Counties! Using knowledge established out west, finding wildlife violators was a breeze. I quickly set records for the numbers of citations issued. (5) Professionally, I was happy.

Within months I started finding articles of men's clothing in my personal car. Tearful denials of infidelity did not fool me. I knew I had a big problem. My wife soon left me for a Forks cop, the same guy that had stood up for me at my courthouse wedding! (6)   Although very sad and humiliated at the time I finally realized that her leaving was the second best thing that had ever happened to me. Becoming a fish cop was number one! I do not recall her ever having an original thought nor do I recall the sound of her voice. She is mentioned here only to point out that I remained prone to mistakes, and to keep my chronology of events intact.

(5) In those days a "toaster" was presented to the Fisheries Officer that wrote the most tickets in a year. (No longer done)

(6) Thirty two years later my former best man was a retired Bremerton Police Detective. He relayed to me through a third party that he was now divorced. I expressed no interest whatsoever at the news. Later I laughed about it. The poor bastard got what he deserved, he no doubt lost half of his police pension. I wonder if she left him for a cop?

***

I went back to work with great enthusiasm. For the first time in my career I routinely, and on a daily basis placed criminals in handcuffs and booked them into jail. Not so much for wildlife crimes but for arrest warrants that other police officers were too busy to serve. I got to the point where I could look at a guy and with a reasonable degree of accuracy predict if he had a warrant. This skill came to me easily as it does with most officers when they start to figure things out.

***

Once while driving by a very seedy looking liquor store I saw something that was not quite right. I circled back for a better look. The clerk was engaged in some sort of combat with a man over the cash register. Without thinking I rushed in. I made a calculated guess as to whom the crook was. I guessed right and applied one of the many "Kung Foo" moves they taught at the academy called a "Yoshida Come-along." It always worked in class so I gave it a try. The move required a perp with longish hair. This feature gave one a superior grip which in turn created more options for control. To my utter amazement it worked. The right guy was in cuffs in less than two seconds. I directed the clerk to dial 911. When I looked down at the bad guy I just about shit my pants. He was face down in a pool of frothy blood. His face looked exactly as if one placed an M-80 fire cracker up both nostrils and lit it. He was screaming over and over "You Cunt, Fuck You." I realized that he was clearly inebriated and that his alcohol intoxication no doubt had something to do with the excessive bleeding. My back up soon arrived. I felt very compelled to explain that I really did not know how the man got so bloody. There was never any blood at police school! The older of the two cops said "yea right" in a very disbelieving way. I truly felt bad. The good news was that the paramedics came and went and the perp was carted off to jail. I was never compelled to write a report, never testified in court and I have no idea what ever happened to the guy.

***

One day, while minding my own business I observed a pickup with Canadian plates back up to a store front. To my surprise a man started pitching salmon into a fish tote on the sidewalk. All of the fish were "cookie cutter", in size and shape. They were all very silver bright and limp, not frozen. The date was approximately July 1st, and it was not an odd numbered year. These observations would have meant very little to most officers, but I got excited. All of these factors in combination convinced me that these fish were Canadian origin sockeye and almost certainly unlawfully taken. I could rule out pink salmon because they only occur locally in odd numbered years. The uniform size and shape ruled out chinook or chum. Troll caught coho salmon were a possibility but the Canadian plates, registered to the interior of British Columbia suggested a Frazier River origin. Sockeye salmon are an early returning fish (July is typical) and Canada's Frazier River boasts some of the largest runs in the world. In this manner I was able, with a reasonable degree of certainty, to identify the product from a distance. A quick radio call confirmed that no state sockeye commercial seasons had opened yet. I was on to something! Having learned from my previous investigative failures I consulted with an old fish cop that had experience with such matters. Together we came up with a plan which was: "Flip the buyer, set up another delivery, make a covert buy, all the while consulting with Canadian authorities." I was overwhelmed, but in actuality this operation was quite simple.

I called a Canadian fisheries officer who stated that there was currently a "First Nations Ceremonial" sockeye fishery taking place on the Frazier River. These fish were not to be sold for commercial purposes. These facts significantly bolstered my suspicions.

I made contact with the buyer who of course had no documentation for the fish which means that he had also committed a crime. I convinced him that assisting me was his best course of action. I had him call the seller and request another load. I arranged for an undercover officer, my sergeant, to pose as a worker while the fish were delivered. Within an hour we were set up for a "buy / bust" two days hence.

I was very excited, my first significant commercial case. I watched as my boss waited on the side walk covertly pushing a broom. Right on que, the perpetrator showed up with a load of contraband sockeye. The suspect unloaded them with the help of the new worker. So focused was the perpetrator on receiving the payment check he did not see my approach and I snatched check out of the suspects hand before the ink was dry. (The ink smudged) The sad part was that two small children and the suspect had to take a bus back to the border.

The Canadians sent down a Federal fish cop who examined the fish. This guy was good. I remember that he collected bits of vegetation still stuck to some of the fish. He was able to identify parts of a rare plant indigenous to an obscure tributary of the Frazier located at the suspected fishing site. I ended up giving testimony in a Canadian Court. All suspects were convicted.

This simple case greatly increased my confidence. I was learning from past mistakes. I was off and running.

***

Urban salmon snagger's are a very different from those of the Forks area. First of all the Forks boys are all white. Urban violators consist of all races. The only similarities being greed and that fact that all are male. The city boys were far more bold and easy to catch. They were more street wise however, no doubt due to more frequent contact with the police. They were emboldened by a common unawareness that fisheries patrol officers even existed. This was not an unreasonable assumption if one considered the fact that here were no more than five fish cops in all of King and Snohomish County combined. (There were an equal number of gamies about, they too worked snagger's, but had a different set of priorities.) The city boys were however far more difficult to deal with. They often fled on foot. Very often they used false names and had fishing licenses borrowed from others. Back on the west end, the boys would not think of a citation going to warrant because everyone in town would hear about it. They would not run from me, or at least very far, because I could just pick them up later. Using a false name was out of the question because no one could keep from laughing if they tried. To the Forks snagger's there was a certain honor to getting pinched, a ritc of passage in a sense. My "good old boy" contact style that usually helped out west was useless here.

***

The Green River, enroute to the Duwamish waterway flows through the Kent Valley. In this area the river appears very unnatural due to human influence. It weaves around guided by rip rap banks, many of which create a place where chinook salmon rest. As is the case with all salmon streams, potential snagging hotspots are obvious.

One night I parked my brand new Chevy Blazer (The best patrol car ever) at a location where I could observe a snag hole that I knew was going to get hit. At the stroke of midnight a small pickup backed under a bridge spanning the river. I waited, giving them time to set up rods and access the snag hole. I heard car doors opening and closing indicating at least two people. In my excitement I misjudged the passage of time and walked to the river bank far too soon. As I approached the truck I noticed two fishing rods set up with snag gear in the back. A man in the driver's seat flipped a joint out the window. My snagging case was totally blown so I decided to "save par" with a marijuana pinch. I ordered the driver out of the car. He complied, but when I told him to turn around and place his hands behind his back he refused. He gave me several indicators that an assault was pending. The most obvious being "Im gonna kick your ass." I drew my ASP (A collapsible impact weapon) and again stated my demand. He laughed and held out a limp wrist, apparently complying. I placed my cuffs on this one wrist. I positioned my hands on the cuffs setting up an "ignition turn". This is another police move that always worked in training. The ignition turn places pressure directly on the wrist bone and works in combination with pain compliance and leverage. With crank of the wrist, a downward pull and a step backwards, the violator always ends up harmlessly face down on the ground. I was emboldened by my previous successful application of the "Yosheda Come-along" and with total confidence employed the move. The man, much smaller than I, laughed out loud. Then he got pissed. He lowered his shoulders and tackled me below my waist. I have no idea how, but my next recollection was that the man was cuffed and laying on the ground. He began screaming like in a cheap horror film. He was hysterical to the point that serious drugs must have been on board. I was still concerned about the other guy who was yet to exit the car. The man's screaming echoed out across the valley. He then started saying that I had broken his spine and that he could not move his legs. At the time I was convinced that this was true. I was scared to death. I made a radio call and within seconds I saw blue and red lights across the valley indicating both a police and EMT response. I approached the man in an attempt to comfort him but his response put me in fear of getting bitten. His legs remained limp but he was still full of fight. I watched as the EMT's secured the man to a spine board and followed as they transported him to the hospital. I escorted the gurney around the hospital and stood by as the man was examined. At some point I recall him being cuffed to the hospital bed. I consulted with the doctor and asked "What kinds of drugs is this guy on?" He mumbled something about "patient doctor privilege" but then told me that the guy's spine was fine and that this whole scene was "bullshit". Greatly relieved, I realized that by faking an injury there would be no way that the jail would accept him for a minor criminal charge which this was, and the hospital would not keep him because he was not injured! I never met a man on the west end of the peninsula that would have sunk to such depths of deceit…It was brilliant. (The man was ultimately convicted of assault.)

I experienced another memorable event at this exact same spot a few days later. This time in broad daylight I observed two men snagging fish. I first made all of the observations sufficient to support a criminal charge then I made contact. Both men cut their terminal gear and tossed the evidence into the river. No big deal, in fact I was glad that they did so because it supported my case by demonstrating culpability, (criminal intent) it also gave me a second criminal charge called "Refuse to submit gear for inspection." I escorted both men up a steep bank. One bolted. I did not give chase because I knew where they were parked and he was likely to return to this vehicle. Basically, had he not returned I would have impounded the car and pinched him later. Sure enough, while writing the other man a citation the runner returned. I placed him in cuffs briefly, justified by his prior and likely to be repeated behavior. I noticed that the man had a very slight scratch on his forehead. The river bank was infested with invasive blackberry plants and the injury was no greater than could be inflicted by a blade of grass. I thought nothing of it. I seem to recall that this man was a non-resident and fishing under an unlawfully held "Resident" license.

Several weeks later I was informed that this man had filed a lawsuit against me for false arrest and assault. The case went to civil court and I was represented by the state.

Court was held in a high-rise building in downtown Seattle. My testimony was very straight forward. The plaintiffs provided a version of events that was almost unrecognizable. They alleged that I had chased the one man and intentionally inflicted injury upon him by striking his head with my pistol. Their offer of proof was a Polaroid snapshot of a bloody forehead. What concerned me most was that their lawyer was a locally famous civil rights attorney. He had pursued numerous high profile cases and had so frequently gone after Seattle Police Officers that the paperwork he submitted regarding my case had "Seattle Police" in all headers. These references had been lined through and replaced with "Washington Department of Fisheries."

The photo showed what may have begun as a scratch but in my opinion it had been aggravated by repeated blows from a hard object. In addition, coagulated blood spread from the wound in three different directions. Impossible in my opinion unless done so intentionally. These suspicions and more came to light. The plaintiff's case was clearly failing. In an act of desperation the plaintiff stood up and pointed a finger in my face. Tearfully, and very dramatically he stated words to the effect that I had hit him with my pistol, and while bleeding I dipped my finger in his wound and licked the blood off my fingers. He then alleged that I was sexually gratified by the experience. One direct quote that I recall was "I gotta know why you did that to me." He also said that the experience was so traumatic that he only now remembered the sordid details. I have never been so shocked in my life.

I remember testifying about having had blood born pathogen training and that such an act would go against my training and my nature. I considered pointing out to the court that there had been no mention of me being naked and having worn a jumpsuit at the time, an erection would have very difficult to spot. I held my tongue.

I survived my first lawsuit but not without a great deal of stress. It would not be the last time.

***

The Green River flows from its relatively pristine source westerly. Ultimately it passes the City of Auburn and a stream called Soos Creek on its way to Puget Sound. It is the home of a very productive Chinook salmon hatchery where I worked briefly as a young man. "Green River" fall chinook stock have been introduced extensively. Almost all Puget Sound hatchery origin fall chinook are descendants of these fish. Their behavioral phenotype includes a tendency to migrate and grow in Canadian waters. (Local anglers, whose taxes pay for their production, ironically must travel to Canada to catch them.)

On their return migration they are also known by discerning local anglers as "non-biters" meaning that they are difficult to catch. Many stage up in Seattle's Elliot Bay. A significant recreational fishery exists for them here. Their harvest numbers are closely watched due to allocations owed to tribes associated with the Point Elliot Treaty. The result being that the recreational fishery in the bay is brief and highly regulated.

The lower end of the Green is called the Duwamish Waterway, flowing through Tukwila, Georgetown and past Harbor Island as a slurry of eco vomit. In spite of this it was home to perhaps the best run of Fall Chinook in the State!

At its lowest point, where it enters Elliot Bay the West Seattle Freeway spans this water course. Directly underneath is the Spokane Street Bridge. Here lies without a doubt the most disgusting fishing hole in America.

I was introduce to this spot by a veteran Game Warden. He knew it well and it was clear to me at the time that he wanted someone to work it with. I soon found out why.

The anglers that frequented this spot scared me. It was unclear where they lived. They were often dropped off sometimes in taxi cabs or just appeared from the shadows. Very criminally sophisticated, they employed counter surveillance techniques far beyond those employed by the Forks boys. These guys were night owls, midnight to 4 A.M. was the busiest time. I collected many weapons from these anglers including cheap pistols, bolo knives, brass knuckles a variety of truncheons and switchblades. I never saw a salmon caught here lawfully although I saw many caught. All were snagged. One advantage that I had was that these folks were not intimidated by being booked into jail. It was only a minor inconvenience for them because they knew that the King County Jail would not hold them for low level crimes. After a quick bus ride they were back. Snagging tickets were more likely than not to slip through the cracks of the courthouse floor and never get filed. Any fine that happened to be imposed would simply be ignored. A warrant may be issued but the local police would not bother serving them because the jails were already far beyond capacity with "real criminals." The end result being that these guys were not afraid of anything that I could do to them. Resisting arrest or kicking my ass, which would have been easy for most, was simply not worth it. I was therefore relatively safe. I recall citing several of the most incorrigible anglers two or three times in the same day.

These guys were good. Landing a fish was problematic due to a 20 foot vertical drop from the fishing platform to sea level. They improvised ring nets, a crab fishing device. When a fish was hooked, this device was expertly dropped down and using heavy line the snagged fish would be dragged into the submerged net. Hand over hand the fish was pulled up killed and inevitably stashed in one of several trash cans or dumpsters nearby. Often the fish would be skirted away in a waiting vehicle before I could react. These anglers had a self-imposed rule. Never admit they had a stashed fish and never admit that a fish was theirs! I don't recall this rule ever being broken.

I annoyed them to a point where the volume of arrests dropped despite an increased number of fish arriving. Changing tactics, I made contact with the owner of a dilapidated warehouse. It was three stories high and had a commanding view of the bridge, this would work. The place was totally without power at night and pitch dark. With a key supplied by the owner, I would enter and climb three flights of hazardous stairs to a window. From this point I would mount a spotting scope and settle in to make observations. This innovation worked very well. The problem was that this building was right out of a horror movie complete with monsters inhabiting all dark corners and stairwells. (7) It took me a while to figure out that homeless people had taken up residence. I was startled by them often but they left me about my business.

***

My efforts saved a few fish to the benefit of the tribal gillnetters fishing directly above and to the throng of snagger's inhabiting the waters nearby the hatchery. This facility always got their required escapement and then some. They would have with or without my efforts. I realize now that my endeavors would have been far more productive someplace else, perhaps in a stream with wild fish. (8)

(8) Sport fishing regulations at the time did not differentiate between wild and hatchery fish.

***

There was one thing that always bothered me about patrolling the Green River valley in 1988. The Green River murders were very much in the news. A suspect, unidentified at the time was known to be a fisherman and at one point a local trapper was a person of interest. I patrolled at night in out of the way locales and often encountered suspicious vehicles with warm engines hidden in the brush along the river. Finding discarded clothing, other refuse and yes, the smell of rotting flesh, was commonplace. I always assumed road kill or discarded fish guts. I was never once contacted by the "Green River Task Force" nor any other agency. Although never briefed as to what to look out for, I constantly recorded license plates and vehicle identification numbers of suspicious cars. I habitually jotted down the names of persons engaging in unexplained activities. Aware that reaching out could put me on a person of interest list I contacted a King County detective and offered my help. I explained my familiarity with the area and my patrol habits. He politely listened made a note to himself and walked away. Who knows what could have been if Fisheries Patrol Officers were considered to be "real police."

Applying Lessons Learned

`

I look up from my writing to the sound of a flower pot breaking. I yell at a deer eating my prize flowers. Several outbursts later the doe moved to the apple tree. At least she listened to me!

I would not have missed my Seattle patrol time for anything in the world. However it was not the place I wanted to be. Thankfully the Olympia fisheries patrol station opened up and I was approached by my dear friend and new supervisor Jim Tuggle. I was flattered and quite surprised when he suggested that I take this station. I had the shallow roots that only a bachelor could have and jumped at the chance.

Having grown up Olympia I was already familiar with all of the streams lakes and shoreline areas of south Puget Sound. I knew the public lands and vast industrial timberlands common to adjacent counties. I felt more than qualified for the change and looked forward to being an effective officer right out of the gate. I hit the ground running and never looked back.

By this time the Washington State Department of Game and the Department of Fisheries were moving rapidly toward merging. In 1994 the state legislature confirmed long term rumors by making it so. This meant that my enforcement priorities would now include game and game fish protection and was no longer limited to food fish enforcement. Also, merger brought to light a need for "general authority" which meant that fish and wildlife officers would be authorized by state law to enforce all criminal laws of the state of Washington. (Yes, that included speeding and drunk drivers, theft, assault and answering police calls in general.) I loved the idea and relished the concept of working with hunters and game fish anglers. I was also one of the few officers who had already been certified by the Criminal Justice Training Commission, most had yet to complete the certification course. From this point forward new hires of the merged agency (Washington Department of Fish and Wildlife) were required to complete CJTC training prior to deployment.

Many of the older gamies were intimidated by the idea of working the very complex commercial fishing regulations and had an aversion to patrolling on the open ocean. (I could sympathize with that.) There was an immediate mass migration to the east side of the state.

***

Enforcement priorities were vastly different between the two groups as were their feelings about treaty hunting and fishing rights. Many of the older gamies never accepted tribal off reservation hunting and fishing despite established U.S. Supreme Court case law. Fish Cops had long since accepted tribal fishing rights and better understood the inevitable that off reservation tribal hunting rights would follow suit. That said the following anecdote may better illustrate the difference in enforcement practices.

The merger of Fisheries and Game was not quite official when I patrolled a favorite trout stream of mine. I encountered a man on Skookum Creek in the month of March. This stream is the epicenter of sea sun cutthroat spawning in South Puget Sound. Cutthroat were and remain protected with a "catch and release" only fishery in marine areas and with complete stream closures during the spawning season (winter / spring) The man was in possession of a dozen or so large cutthroat. I detained him and asked a few questions. I determined that this man, who lived in a nearby creek side home, poached these fish habitually. I soon learned that he had an unknown number of these "brood stock" trout in his home. I conducted a search of a chest freezer with the man's consent. I discovered a frozen mass of cutthroat of all sizes, impossible to count. I estimated the combined weight at about 100 pounds! Yes, all of the fish were taken unlawfully from the closed waters of Skookum Creek.

Thrilled with my discovery and aware that the local gamie may be interested I called him on a bag phone. (9) He quickly responded and was very clearly interested in my find. However, what caught his eye was a single ¼ pound package labeled "elk steak 2/14."

He called his boss, an old school gamie who especially disapproved of tribal hunting and fish cops in general. At the sergeant's direction my new partner inquired of the suspect the source of the suspiciously dated elk steak. A good question, because general elk seasons would have been closed on the date 2/14. The suspect freely admitted that he had been given the steak by a tribal friend. After all, he explained, it's not like it was poached! (Which it wasn't.) Unbelievably, the sergeant then instructed my partner to cite the man for "possession of game meat without a statement" and to issue a verbal warning for the genocide of a significant portion of Skookum Creek's wild trout population! This decision was made only because of the tribal origin of the single steak! I remain to this day shocked and angry that this form of bias was tolerated...by anyone!

(9) The forerunner to the cell phone it weighed about 10 pounds and could be carried with a shoulder strap. They were only marginally functional.

***

The Vail Tree Farm is a large tract of industrial timberland located in S.E. Thurston and N. Lewis counties. It was here that I was introduced to big game enforcement.

The land owner would open a few access gates and allow pubic hunting on weekends during the modern firearm deer season. This area supported large numbers of deer. The clear cuts, interconnected with a vast road system made for good hunting. It was typical for 2,500 cars to access this area from a single main gate before 7 a.m. (Assuming an average occupancy of two hunters per car, at least 5,000 hunters per day hunted here.) There were only two ways in and two ways out. Entry and exit gates were manned. The Department of Fish and Wildlife operated a biological check station on the busiest intersection of logging spurs. Hunters were required to stop as biological data was collected. Successful hunters were photographed with their trophies and Polaroid snapshots were posted on a brag board for all to see. It was the epicenter of deer hunting in my world. A carnival atmosphere prevailed, it was a lot of fun. (10)

Often hunters would report violations to the biologists manning the check station. (11) I tended to patrol nearby so to respond to what were often easy pinches. Most of these violations involved improper tagging. Often a report involving the unlawful take of a doe would come in. These cases were more difficult to solve due to difficulties describing locations. Even reports including a suspect's license plate were problematic due to the digits being obscured by dirt and mud. It was a lot of fun sorting through the reports and prioritizing those that were solvable in the short term.

Hunting regulations prohibit the possession of a "loaded long gun in a motor driven vehicle." A loaded long gun is defined as a shotgun or rifle with attached ammunition. Not necessarily one with a live round in the firing chamber. The rifles with a "tubed" round were the ones that scared me. All hunters are taught at their required hunter education class the dangers and illegalities of having such a gun. This law is often ignored by impatient and unethical hunters who want to be ready if a buck appears in the roadway. Often as I approached hunters inside vehicles, they would panic and frantically start ejecting live rounds in an effort to avoid a $250 ticket. This act was especially obvious with lever guns (lever action) due to the exaggerated arm movement required to eject a round, and were especially dangerous. Each time a round is ejected another is inserted into the firing chamber as the rounds are cycled out. The gun could easily discharge if a finger was inadvertently on the trigger. A Washington state game warden was once killed this way and I know of several incidents where rifles were fired inside a car. Loaded rifles were not tolerated. I never recall issuing a warning for this violation. LLGIMDV citations were my bread and butter while working this popular hunting area. (12)

(10) All hunters were essentially captive, and were forced to pass at least one wildlife officer prior to exiting the unit.

(11) Affectionately referred to by officers as "Bugs"

(12) Loaded long gun in a motor driven vehicle.

***

One term used by fish and wildlife officers is "honey deer." Macho deer hunters, particularly early in the season would shoot a smallish buck when they were really after one they could brag about. Unwilling to put their own tag on a small buck, which would effectively end their hunting season, they would often use a tag issued to a wife or associate who may or may not be present. Often this common criminal conspiracy would involve a phone call home that went something like this:

"Honey, you just killed a buck. Go buy a deer tag and meet me at the Vail check station."

Here's one of many memorable Vail tree farm, "Honey Deer" cases:

As I was engaging a group of friendly hunters at the check station two vehicles pulled in. One was a very dirty 4x4 Dodge pickup driven by an elderly man, the other was a relatively clean economy car of some kind occupied by two elderly females wearing hair curlers and pajamas. I noted that the elderly male driving the truck was very dirty and covered with dried blood. His pickup contained three dead buck deer, including two very small "spikes" and one much larger three point. All were tagged as required. Predictably, the two smaller bucks had been tagged with documents issued to the women and the largest with a tag issued to the man. The women's tags were dated with a purchase time of 8 a.m. today. (It was only 9:30 a.m.) The group had only one rifle between them. Trying very hard to stifle a laugh I explained to the man my suspicions. He insisted that the group had each killed a deer. (This lie, in and of itself is a wildlife crime.) He even added details and laughed about how many shots each woman had taken compared to his one and only "clean kill shot." I approached the two women and conducted the easiest interrogation of my life. "Where's your rifles?" They both blurted out that they had warned the husband and "brother in law" that they would never get away with this. Written statements were collected.

I then returned to the now very nervous husband. He waffled a little but stuck to his story. I called over Sergeant Makoviney (my brother in law) who had been enjoying watching this scene play out. He kept a straight face and played along as I explained to him the circumstances in the presence of the suspect. Sergeant Mack was smoking a cigar at the time and looked for all the world like Buford T. Justice. He barked a well-timed and very dramatic one word comment. "Bullshit." and walked away. The husband broke, and admitted to killing all three deer and to his role as instigator of this honey deer conspiracy. (13)

(13) All three violators pled guilty to numerous license fraud charges, and criminal conspiracy. The deer were *seized* a hefty fine was imposed on each. All hunting privileges were revoked for two years.

***

42

The Webster's were a local hunter / gatherer group that lived near my home in N.E. Olympia. Consisting of entirely males, this dysfunctional family inhabited the home of an elderly grandfather. All were avid hunters and fisherman. William, the son of the patriarch was a trained meat cutter and convicted felon. (14) The grandsons, all had different mothers according to one. None of the able bodied Webster's had jobs. It appeared that the elderly head of household supported all.

Several members of this family had shot our fake deer a few times and all were documented wildlife violators. A Gamie had received a tip from a man, stating that the Webster's had five unlawful deer and an elk in their home currently. This was very believable information and clearly something to follow-up on. The problem being that the reporting party was also a habitual poacher and therefore his voracity would not hold up to the scrutiny required to validate a search warrant. This kind of investigation was new to me so I played a secondary role.

A more experienced wildlife officer said that we were going to pull a "phone fuck." He explained to me that he would have a female voice call the Webster's at a time when we knew they were all home and say " You don't know me but I just overheard the game wardens planning to serve a search warrant at your home tonight at 7 pm.," and hang up. The plan was that officers would all be in position observing the home and make a traffic stop on any vehicle leaving if it appeared that deer or elk meat was hastily loaded into it. A search of the car would reveal the contraband.

Although beautifully simple, I questioned the legality of this plan. I also did not think it would work. Quite frankly I felt that no one was that dumb! I was assured that the prosecutor had signed off and that this plan had worked many times in the past. And besides that, I was told, the one brother had "shot the decoy deer twice and was more than dumb enough!"

I set up in the chase car and was assigned to stop any vehicle leaving with deer or elk meat. I was notified the moment the ruse phone call was made. Immediately thereafter I heard loud profanity coming from the Webster's home. The old double wide was rocking on its foundation. Between partially drawn curtains I saw numerous men frantically putting together cardboard boxes and running about. Another officer with a view of the rear door reported that several men were loading boxes and an un-cut rear quarter of an elk into a van. I started my patrol truck and prepared for the inevitable chase. The van entered the roadway, I activated my emergency lights (Somebody finally got around to showing me how.) I recall approaching the car and seeing an elk quarter in plain view along with the boxes of meat.

The Webster's were a very strange and interesting bunch of poachers. Unlike most, they always told the truth once the gig was up. They always dutifully paid the court imposed fines and willingly served their short jail sentences. Albeit a little out of character, they never gave up the female voice warning them of our phony search warrant plans. They never suspected that the call was a ruse.

This was not the last "rodeo" for the Webster clan. A Grays Harbor based wildlife officer made a similar case at the same home a few years later. Years after that, I recovered a closed season doe and 13 unlawful firearms at the same residence. William remembered me and once again provided a written confession. Convicted of yet another felony, he received a lifetime hunting revocation in Washington as well as in 44 other states. He was also plagued with a series of fishing violations over the years. I could not resist the temptation and told him about the "ruse" telephone call used on him years prior. He did not believe me.

(14) I later learned that this prior felony conviction "grand larceny" was for cattle rustling.

***

I had befriended a very active Washington state trooper who had an interest in fish and wildlife crimes. One December night, well after midnight he called me at home. He told me that he had just arrested and processed a drunk driver on interstate five. "So what?" I said. "Well, the suspect's car contains too many steelhead to count …and a gill net." Suddenly very interested, I promised to visit the impound yard in the morning where the car was secured.

I arrived to find several dozen very large steelhead strewn about the back seat of the car and a section of gill net. Oddly there was also a kitchen sink in the back seat! Clearly the fish had been very hastily placed inside, which was consistent with the fact that heavy drinking was involved.

Steelhead are a game fish. That means they cannot be lawfully commercially taken unless harvested in a "treaty Indian gillnet fishery". I found it suspicious that the drunk driver was traveling north bound on I-5 in Olympia while in possession of commercial quantities of fish.

Steelhead returning to rivers south of Olympia are outside the usual and accustomed fishing areas of treaty tribes. Traveling northbound through Olympia with uncleaned steelhead was suspicious in itself. Even lawful sport caught fish would need to be formally documented and the lawful possession limit would be two fish each. The fish were in rigor mortis and not gutted indicating a very recent time of death. They were all large, 12 pounds or better, and very silver bright. Something about these observations clicked, these fish looked very familiar to me.

As a young man I worked at the Cowlitz Salmon Hatchery. While stationed there I became a very intense steelhead fisherman. As an angler and student of fish, I was very familiar with the fish culture practices and steelhead program at the Cowlitz Trout Hatchery. At the time hatchery steelhead were not mass marked. Even without a clipped fin, to a hatchery man, indications of hatchery origin are obvious. The rays in the dorsal fins are shorter than those of wild fish and there was always slight bending of the first few fin rays. Both lobes of the tail would be similarly slightly eroded unlike wild fish. Lastly, Cowlitz Trout Hatchery was the only hatchery in the state that raised steelhead that tended to spend an extra year at sea and thus larger than other hatchery fish. Twelve pounders would most likely be what we called "three salts", steelhead that lived three years in a marine environment instead of the more typical two years. In this case the lack of any fin clips was another indication of Cowlitz origin.

Putting together all of these observations I was well on my way to establishing a "circumstantial" unlawful gillnetting case on the Cowlitz River.

I still had work to do to prove my theory. DNA analysis was not available to me at the time although I looked into it having had experience identifying salmon stocks through tissue analysis. I had also collected thousands of scales from sport caught fish and seemed to recall that hatchery fish would show an unusually wide first growth ring in each scale. I brought the fish to the head biologist who had expertise with Cowlitz steelhead stock. He examined the fish and their scales. Using the same deductive reasoning employed by me, but with a far better ability to articulate it, he concluded that the fish were most likely of Cowlitz Hatchery origin.

Further investigation established that the occupants of the car, and the drunk driver were Muckleshoot tribal fishers. Perhaps they felt justified gillnetting the Cowlitz, perhaps it was! For sure however gillnetting steelhead in the Cowlitz was unlawful and I am reasonably sure that's what they did. Charges were filed. The cases went to warrant and eventually fell through the cracks of the courthouse floor. I do believe however, that in this case, some measure of justice was served. The typical penalties for DUI were far beyond those associated with a fishing case.

***

A land owner called me reporting gun shots at night near his home. In this part of the county such calls usually meant nothing but in this case the caller seemed credible and was able to associate the shots with probable deer hunting. I was interested. The reporting party (R.P.) explained that after the three shots he observed an older blue Ford Bronco enter his access road after crashing through thick brush down a forested hillside. He described conspicuous overhead lights and body damage to the vehicle. I responded the next morning with my boss at the time, Sergeant Dan Brinson. Tracking the path the suspect vehicle in reverse we found ourselves on an overgrown logging spur that once accessed state forest land. After a bit of rough off road driving we found what appeared to be drag marks in the brush in an area of 're-prod." (Five to ten year old fir trees that had been replanted after logging.) We found fresh blood and deer hair associated with the drag marks. Now we had something, a closed season deer kill but no dead deer or suspects.

At this point we knew we had a crime but little else. We did what all police officers do, we brain stormed a profile of the violator. We guessed that drugs were involved, probably meth which was rampant in rural areas at the time. The reckless act in the attempt to escape the area by intentionally crashing through the trees supported this theory. We also assumed that the suspects were locals. Who else would know about the shortcut through the brush? While poking along the drag marks we found tire tracks right where the blood ended, indicating that an animal was loaded into a vehicle. Most interesting was a small area of debris consisting of bits of paper, cigarette butts and several empty cans of cheap malt liquor. The same brand that Sergeant Brinson and I often drank together. We carefully examined a piece of paper and discovered that it was an expired proof of insurance card displaying a vehicle identification number and a name! Our excitement was short lived because the document was years old and displayed an address hundreds of miles away. We couldn't even be sure that it was associated with the suspect vehicle.

After a few phone calls. (Officers did not have lap top computers in their cars in those days and had to do their sleuthing using their wits.) We learned that the vehicle identification number was in fact that of a blue 1974 Ford Bronco! This fact confirmed the reporting party's voracity. If we could find this vehicle we were on to something.

I called a friendly WSP dispatcher, with expertise in such matters. These highly trained professionals always amazed me with their competence. They can not only multi task like a jet fighter pilot, they could always anticipate what I needed even though I often could not articulate it. In this case she explained that my suspect vehicle had been sold and resold numerous times. She was able to provide an address where the vehicle was last registered that was only about three miles away. I recall being amazed that anyone could be that smart. Sergeant Brinson and I were off and running.

The address was located in a notorious drug area in south Thurston County. Ramshackle single wide trailers interspersed with piles of garbage and abandoned cars were strewn about. Stray cats, tipped over garbage cans and drug paraphernalia in the streets confirmed our original profile. Few of the homes had visible house numbers but one especially dumpy abode was located where the house numbers should have matched the address that we had. We called out our location and approached this home, all the while scanning the area for the home bred pit bull dragging a length of chain that always seemed to occupy such places.

We knocked on the door. I heard movement and hushed voices inside. Eventually a young woman opened the door just a crack. I made a very general inquiry about a blue Ford Bronco. Of course she was unaware of the existence of any such vehicle. I engaged her in conversation as long as I could. All the while picking up on clear deception but the woman gave up nothing. Upon leaving Dan and I both knew that we would be back, we just needed to develop a plan.

Several times later in the day we cruised the area looking for the suspect Bronco, each time going by this same home. At one point we engaged a small boy in conversation. He told us about a man climbing out of the back window of the very same home this morning, about the same time that we were knocking on the door!

We were getting close. We decided to conduct yet another door knock. The same woman came to the door. Once again I explained what we were looking for. She made the mistake of trying to explain why a man had climbed out her window this morning...she had been burglarized! She did not bother to call the cops, nor did she feel compelled to tell us about it during our prior visit!

Police Officers know that when a story makes no sense that it is a deception. While pointing this out as tactfully as I could a very large woman pulled up in a very small car. I recall the car's leaf springs violently relaxing as she stepped out. She kept her distance but could not have been more obviously listening to what I was saying. I ignored her and continued my questioning. Although not true, I planted the seed in the minds of all present that I had identified the boyfriend and that an arrest warrant would be issued later in the day. I did this knowing that the suspect would receive this false tip, hoping that it would flush him out.

Several minutes later, I terminated the interview. I said to Dan, "Do you realize what just happened?" "No, what?" "It's the old send the fat girl over to see what the cops know trick. I'm telling you that's what just happened. I got her license plate, let's drive by her house, were gonna find that Bronco, were gonna make this case!" I must admit that I had never seen this trick executed before but I saw many variations of the same trick later.

Dispatch provided an address associated with this new information and within minutes we were there. No one appeared to be home but fresh tire tracks in the uncut grass led directly to a vehicle covered in a brand new blue tarp. It still had the creases associated with the neat folds placed in it at the factory. We could see the telltale shape of a Ford Bronco underneath it as well as those of the conspicuous overhead running lights described by the reporting party. I love it when a plan comes thru!

I did not have a search warrant but home bred pit bulls could not have kept me from looking under that tarp. After all, the vehicle and all of the potential evidence contained within could have easily been driven away. Also the likely presence of firearms and a person who knows how to use them justified the warrantless search. It was a frisk for weapons in my mind at the time. Only a police officer would understand my rationale. The engine block was warm and I observed two scoped rifles, a hand held spotlight and an un-gutted doe deer inside. A search warrant for the vehicle was executed later.

My memory of the rest of this story is clouded. I recall speaking with one of the suspects on the phone and negotiating with him to surrender himself. Ultimately he confessed and gave up his partner in crime.

***

Patrolling in the south sound area brought me very close to the shellfish farming industry. A huge part of our patrol duties involved enforcing associated Department of Health regulations. Commercial harvest can only lawfully occur in certified areas. Unfortunately there are massive amounts of easily accessible clams in many polluted areas. These dirty clams often enter the black market and are distributed retail, and wholesale, through the back door. Local infamous harvest sites for dirty clams included Bremerton's Dyes Inlet and Olympia's Budd Inlet. (15)   Fish and wildlife officers familiar with these areas never order clams in a restaurant. We nervously laughed at those who did.

There are numerous potential victims. Those eating the dirty clams may get sick or die, and the reputation of the legitimate shellfish industry is damaged by each incident. Also, dirty clams may be distributed across the country which greatly increases the risk. (16)

We made many dirty clam cases over the years, often patrolling known polluted beaches during nighttime low tides. I once observed two men harvest 400 pounds of clams in an hour and hide the clams, and themselves, fifty feet up the lower end of a sewer pipe! Had this product not been intercepted, who knows? It's impossible to assess how much contaminated product got past us. No doubt many thousands of pounds.

These cases were very satisfying. I very much enjoyed the heavy labor involved in destroying the potentially toxic product.

Over time I got the distinct impression that we were getting a handle on dirty clams getting into the legitimate market. The problem was that they were still easy to traffic door to door to a variety of small business. My partner and I once made a significant bust and quickly "flipped" the harvester who agreed to make a few controlled sales for us.   (Identical to buy bust operations associated with illegal drugs.) This type of operation required reaching out to our Special Investigation Unit. We gave the case to them and offered our assistance. Ultimately we learned that dirty clams were being sold to numerous restaurants and Ma and Pa grocery stores. Not at all surprising to us, but shocking to many, we determined that some manicure and nail shops were buying and distributing dirty clams as well... Nail shops?

One such joint dealt in high interest loans, sold pornography and distributed dirty clams. I recall that while conducting the raid, with officers in full uniform in plain view, a load of "Bremerton Browns" were delivered.

I'll never forget an associated sound bite on a local TV station made by our Deputy Chief. I told him later that it was that it was the politically correct understatement of the year.

"If you buy your seafood at a nail shop, it's probably an illegal product."

I would have said, "I would sooner eat the clipped fingernails than the clams sold at this shop."

(15) *Often these cases were not charged in local courts, I often speculated that elected officials were understandably trying to protect the integrity of a significant local industry.*

(16) *We referred to these clams as "Turd Clams, Bremerton Browns or Barfers". Shellfish products distributed by legitimate local companies are of very high quality and safe to eat.*

***

Any description of Fish and Wildlife enforcement work in the State of Washington would be incomplete without writing about the recreational razor clam fishery. Only occurring on coastal beaches and available on extreme low tides razor clams drive a prolific recreational opportunity worth millions of dollars each year to area businesses. Well managed by WDFW, this resource adds a great deal to Pacific Northwest values and to the overall quality of life in Washington. Highly regulated, this fishery is relatively easy to manage. Biologists closely track their abundance, reproduction and growth rates and can therefor easily calculate the numbers that can be harvested. Factors that control harvest are the weather, naturally occurring bio toxins, the number of suitable low tides and allocations set aside for treaty tribal harvest. The end result is that clam digging on the Washington coast is open about twenty days each year. (Highly variable)

Although many regulations are in print surrounding this fishery, one is most significant. The daily limit is 15 clams regardless of size or condition. Here in lies the rub. Digging is quite easy, even for a novice digger. Reaching the daily limit is the norm. Almost all diggers go home happy.

The limit itself is quite liberal in that 15 clams provides about two full meals for a hungry man, more for children or those who don't like them as much. Most people find the digging process so much fun that they can't resist digging after a limit is retained. It's like a grown up Easter egg hunt. Who would think of limiting the number of chocolate eggs that a kid would put in his Easter basket! Greed often comes into play. Clam diggers rationalize overages by assisting others who they deem to be less competent diggers, or by digging for relatives left at home who would also like to eat some. Many folks, especially locals have a sense of entitlement to the clams and think that because they missed the last tide that they are entitled to two limits today! Lastly, if a small or damaged clam is dug, it is very easy for many to rationalize discarding it in exchange for a larger undamaged clam.

After accounting for all of these potential rationales to exceed the limit of 15, clam managers have wisely and incontrovertibly published in the regulation pamphlet language that says "The daily limit is the first 15 clams dug, regardless of size or condition."

Discarding clams, or "Wastage" as Fish and Wildlife Officers call it, is so prevalent that biologists often inspect the beach during a dig so that they can calculate the numbers of clams lost in this way. Some speculate that if "wastage" was prevented totally, an entire additional day of digging could be authorized. A million or so dollars of additional revenue for the local economy! Lost also is the almost incalculable monitory value of an individual's outing to the beach!

Fair warning, if an adult digs a razor clam and discards it in view of a Fish and Wildlife Officer, that person will probably get a ticket!

Straight up greed is what officers on the beach are really looking for. I have seen it all from extra limits concealed in children's car seats and diaper bags, to clams stashed down the front of pants. The art of "boot legging", hiding extra clams inside ones boots, may have been invented in Ocean Shores Washington. Stashing clams in spare tire wells, or inside door panels of cars is commonplace. Few local hotel room bath tubs have not been used as receptacles for contraband clams. Many other stealthy tactics are used by clam thieves. Unfortunately many work, largely because we don't have enough officers in the field.

***

One day I was patrolling the Ocean Shores beaches with a veteran officer who was far more experienced than I at the time. We were both observing diggers with high powered spotting scopes waiting for something to happen. We both had made note of clams being discarded and passed off to others but we were after bigger fish this day. My partner says to me, "You see that guy with the red hat? I just watched him drop off a limit of clams at his car and he is now after his second limit." We both watched from a distance of several hundred yards as the man dug a second limit and once again stashed them at his car. He returned to the beach after changing his coat and hat. He resumed digging. With a great deal of interest we switched out attention to this man and totally forgot about the other minor violations that we were watching. Twice more the man returned to the car, dropped off clams and resumed digging, each time changing his appearance. This was gonna be good! On his last trip to the car the man casually removed his boots. We watched as he removed several additional clams from them. We knew that he had at least 4 limits at his car but possibly many more. We decided to make contact. The problem was that we did not see exactly where he had placed each load. We knew that they were in the car, a full sized van, but not the exact location. No problem, they couldn't be too hard to find.

We made contact and advised the man to produce the contraband clams. With confidence and a smirk he said that he had 15 clams only but we were free to search his car if we wished. We would have searched the car with or without permission. Together we looked under seats, in side door panels and in the spare tire well. We made sure that the spare itself was not deflated and sliced open so that it could contain clams. We even removed the old style ash trays from the doors, the ones that would snap out. This afforded us a look inside the walls of the van. No clams! I recall looking inside the gas tank, tapping hub caps and searching the engine compartment, nothing! I was starting to panic and I'm sure my partner was worried too. He had the idea to crawl under the van and inspect the under carriage. We also probed the surrounding area looking for buried clams, all without success. "You wanna borrow my glasses?" the suspect said while stifling a smirk. We were mortified! With every ounce of our pride now gone we felt compelled to retreat, but not without telling the suspect that we knew he was guilty.

Fully expecting a citizen complaint we both began rehearsing what we would be telling the lieutenant within about 12 hours. As always we decided on telling the truth which guaranteed that we would be second guessed for the rest of our lives and retrained as a result. When we had driven about a mile down the beach my partner says "Go Back! I think I know where the clams are."

"Are you sure? We are getting beefed for sure and I need another one like I need a hole in my head."

"Go back, trust me! Remember when I went under the van? Well, I'm pretty sure I saw two mufflers."

"Are you telling me the extra clams are hidden in a fake muffler?"

"They gotta be!"

"Are you sure you don't have double vision?"

"If I did I'd have seen four mufflers!"

"If they are not in the muffler, it's been nice working with you...NOT!

We turned around to find the van under way and entering traffic on the highway. We pulled it over. My partner crawled underneath once again. I saw his feet start to twitch as he was clearly struggling with something. He emerged with a face full of clam juice a clam in one hand and a smile a mile wide.

The Great Fake Muffler Caper was over.

***

Another memorable razor clam case was actually a huge blunder. On this day the weather was fine and the digging great. The season closed at noon but the clams were still showing. Almost all diggers were done for the day having retained their limits hours prior. It was now about 12:30 and only two people remained digging. We watched as limit after limit was ferried to a nearby car. Not only was the season now closed, these folks, a man and wife it turns out, were showing no signs of stopping. I recall losing count of the individual limits that they placed inside the trunk of their car. They were not being innovative, there was no attempt to be sneaky, they displayed no hast at all. They just could not stop digging.

While talking this over with my partner we both became perplexed as to what we were watching. A part of us wanted to see how far over the limit these guys would go, the other part speculated that perhaps someone was forcing them to do this. Still another thought was that perhaps they were digging for commercial purposes and trying to make some money. We were parked in two marked patrol vehicle no more than 200 feet away, what's up with this?

My partner suddenly said, "We fucked up. We should be stopping this carnage not watching it happen." He was right. Up until now I had never really been in this kind of situation. We could make a great point with the courts with two limits over. There were no others involved so it was not like we needed additional evidence. What were we thinking?

We put an end to this crime by issuing tickets and seizing all clams. It turns out these newlyweds were on their honeymoon at the beach. What were they thinking?

When the matter came before the local judge, an avid digger and advocate for razor clam populations, he chewed us both out for letting this happen. This ass chewing was well deserved and it should have been a lot worse. The culprits began a $5,000 payment plan…each!

Thirty three years later while in the Grays Harbor Courthouse I ran into this old judge's son. This man was the current Superior Court judge. I told him this story and felt compelled to apologize. Better late than never.

***

I wrote many search warrants over the years. I found it fun but at first was intimidated by the process. Basically all that has to be done is that an officer must articulate probable cause to believe that a crime has occurred and that evidence of this crime is located in the area to be searched. This belief is presented in writing. If the officer is reasonable, truthful and believable based on one's training, experience and voracity, the warrant is almost always signed by the presiding judge. Most of my search warrants were an effort to locate game meat, fish, firearms, ammunition, cell phone data or bank records. These are all things that fish and wildlife officers look for and judges expect it. A few times I brought search warrant applications to judges seeking things that they had never seen or in some cases never heard of.

While on a routine patrol I drove by a small salmon producing stream. It was mid-summer but for some reason the creek was running brown and very high. I got out to look at the very turbid water. In the distance I heard the sounds of heavy equipment. Knowing that the activity was upstream of my current location I speculated that local developers were shortcutting a few eco permits. My problem was that the suspected site was well within posted private property on a known wetland.

Wetlands are an impediment to land development. "Draining the swamp" is a term that currently means eliminating factors that hold back business potential. Originally it meant literally "draining the swamp" in order to maximize the useful acreage of a person's property or for mosquito control. In the literal sense the negative ecological impacts are enormous. Although many governmental agencies claim to watchdog this process, only one, the Department of Fish and Wildlife has associated criminal laws.

A search warrant would be required for me to gain access. I was not 100 percent sure that the wetland was being unlawfully violated and I hold myself far above the lawful threshold of 51 percent certainty. I needed to know damn well before I bothered a judge, or a land owner for that matter. I drove a short distance to the enforcement hanger and requested a quick flight over the area. Camera in hand I confirmed that unlawful encroachment upon the wetland was occurring. Heavy equipment was currently draining the wetland. So what was it that I needed to recover in a search warrant you ask? Well, when enforcing Fish and Wildlife Hydraulics Codes, it's important that I prove that this body of water is a fish bearing stream. I wanted a warrant first of all to catch the perpetrator in the act but more importantly to collect fish that I knew would be present. I knew that If I did not collect any fish that the defendant would claim that this was not a fish bearing body of water and therefore not a crime.

When I entered the judge's chambers with my affidavit and application I was nervous. This superior court judge probably signed several search warrants per week but I was certain, never one like this. I suggested to the judge that once I gain access I would be collecting fish with dip nets, a 12 foot beach seine and hook and line. I was reasonably certain that I would recover cutthroat trout, wild juvenile coho salmon, stickleback, sculpins and my poster child, the only endemic fish to the State of Washington, the Olympic Mud Minnow. The judge signed my warrant without blinking but her statement to me as I was leaving caused me a little concern. "Good Luck!" as if to say "Your gonna need it."

I assembled a handpicked team of fisheries technicians and a couple of officers. All of the species that I suggested were easily collected from a wet bog that most people would not consider to be fish habitat. Bringing a rod a reel allowed us to collect a single six inch cutthroat from a small opening in the weeds that could not have been netted. Numerous sensitive species of amphibians were also captured and photographed along with hundreds of fish, exactly matching the species composition that I suggested in the warrant! I was able to put together a chargeable case. The only thing left to do was to convince the local prosecutor that a crime had occurred.

This type of investigation is not nearly as common as it should be, but very important. Not only were the fish present at the time saved, both within the excavated area and far below it, the future productivity of an entire drainage was saved from certain destruction. All of my game cases combined had far less positive ecological impact than did this single four hour operation.

I deeply regret not focusing more time to enforcing habitat protection laws.

***

Another odd ball case deserves mentioning. Telemetry tags are designed to be surgically placed inside an adult salmon. This tag emits an electronic signal allowing fisheries biologists to track the fish's movements so that migration data can be collected. There was a project underway on a nearby river were a small number of adult chinook salmon were so tagged and tracked. Technicians walked the stream daily, documenting contact with individual fish using a receiver that captured the telemetry signal. One of these employees called me and explained that he was getting a "Hit" on one of his tags that was emanating from a house on the river. "Are you sure" I asked? "Damn sure" it's coming from inside the kitchen area on the N.E. corner of the house, he said. The river was closed to fishing at the time so if the fish had been caught I should be able to find evidence of illegal fishing.

I wrote a search warrant looking for this particular tag in that particular home. Of course I had to explain to the judge something that was new to her. I recall saying that there was a remote possibility that the tagged fish had died and that perhaps the tag was picked up by someone as a curio and taken home. I thought this very unlikely but possible. Once again the judge quickly signed the warrant and like they always seem to do wished me luck.

I drove to the home in question not knowing what to expect. Unsure of myself, a little paranoid if you will, I went by myself. I wanted my direct supervisor to have a little plausible deniability. I needn't have worried.

As I pulled into the driveway with warrant in hand, a man ran out of the house and greeted me. With a smile on his face he held out the 3 inch tag that I was looking for and said. "Are you looking for this?" Dumbfounded I said "How did you know." He said "I have been expecting someone, just not a cop." This well informed backyard biologist had found a dead fish with this device inside. He had in fact collected it as a curio and called the phone number printed on the tag. A fact that the biologist had not bothered to tell me.

The really strange thing about this was that a week later I recovered a second telemetry tag from another home on this same river! I did not write a search warrant for that one. A man had picked it up after finding a dead salmon on the bank. I now wonder how many of these fish survive this operation at all. At least two out of twelve of the ESA listed fish tagged in this way died as a direct result of attempts to save them.

If a fisherman had killed the two fish, he would have been in trouble.

Urbanized

The Urban Game Warden is expected to deal with injured and problem wildlife. Often such calls would dominate our day. Springtime bears, occasional cougar and deer hit by cars were events that we expect and planed for. Usually an injured deer prompts a call to headquarters and we would be dispatched to the scene. Deer make poor medical patients and nothing but humanely dispatching them is feasible. We all carried .22 caliber rifles for that purpose. I hated this task, the only thing worse for me was the thought of <u>not</u> doing it. The vision of an injured deer dying in a ditch bothers me greatly. Other police agencies would request our assistance with these calls. It was understood that if <u>they</u> discharged their firearm inside the city limits a formal report and shooting investigation would have to be done. Not so with us.

Often these calls prove problematic. The animals would be along busy freeways, near or inside buildings. Many times injured animals would be taken home, laid out on a kitchen floor and given first aid. (17) Often my crisis intervention skills were tested by very upset and compassionate people who would offer to pay any associated vet bills, regardless of cost. I became quite skilled at convincing these folks that a bullet to the brainstem was the best form of euthanasia, as good as even the most expensive veterinarian drugs. (18) It is an urban myth that Fish and Wildlife Officers carry euthanasia drugs for the purposes of putting down injured wildlife. The public would not tolerate the cost.

I recall an injured deer in the meridian of I-5 during rush hour. Troopers were concerned about an inevitable crash because the animal was trying unsuccessfully to cross the freeway. Arriving at the scene it was clear to me that a gunshot was not feasible given the circumstances. At my request the skilled troopers expertly preformed both a northbound and southbound rolling slowdown which provided me the moment I needed to make the shot.

Car accidents involving deer represent real danger to human safety. Bear, cougar and wolves do not. One wouldn't know it based upon the amount of money the state spends to control the latter.

(17) Well-meaning but disconnected animal lovers would inevitably mistake the symptoms of deep traumatic shock for those of gratitude.

(18) We were trained by the WDFW veterinarian to make this point.

***

An injured deer call in downtown Olympia was far more complicated. When I got there Olympia's finest were on scene and doing a great job of keeping the public clear. The problem was that a full sized fire engine was parked near the deer with helmeted

70

firefighters watching the show.   A large crowd had formed. The animal was in a very difficult spot. I was very concerned about a "thru and thru" bullet which may ricochet off the concrete. I was unwilling to take that risk. I wanted to wait until the crowd had dispersed but there was little chance of that. I knew that I would have to make one perfect shot. Like a basketball player at the free throw line with an opportunity to win the championship game, I stepped up to the line. The animal was still trashing around and each time I took aim one of the firefighters watching from the fire truck yelled out, "No, not like that" and "You gotta get 'em in the head." Yeah, no shit Sherlock, I thought to myself. I was getting pissed at the guy. This heckling continued and my concentration was compromised. Finally I turned to this guy and said quite loudly, "Don't tell me how to dispatch a deer, and I won't tell you how to get a cat out of a fucking tree!"   The cops laughed, the fire fighters didn't. I made the shot and left.

**

I live in quiet part of NE Olympia about two miles from the State Capitol Building. One day I received a call from dispatch reporting a cougar just down the street. I had been getting similar calls for days and essentially wrote them off as just another big orange house cat or the pet lynx "Rufus" that escaped from its pen from time to time. This call was different. The female reporting party stated that she came from a hunting family and had seen cougars up close. She ran a day care service and insisted that she would not have made the call had a cougar not been on her porch. Minutes later I arrived and looked around. I walked past a sandbox and swing set. I recall finding among the footprints of children an indistinct single track that was of suspicious size and shape. I walked past a patch of brambles and for some reason looked inside. An adult cougar exploded out of the brush, made contact with my legs and climbed a tree a few feet away. I was shocked to say the least. The trees branches were far too small to support the weight of the 100 pound animal for long. Standing my ground, no more than 8 feet away I called Sergeant Tuggle on my portable radio. I explained my situation as best as I could while holding the cat at gunpoint. I told him that it would be an easy pistol shot but he had to make a decision soon because the branches were about to break and there was a kids t-ball game underway across the street. I was unaware of the numerous homeowners watching the show. I didn't have time to explain everything. The boss made the decision to kill the cat.

I took a deep breath and carefully aimed at the animal's forehead which was no more than 8 feet away and slightly elevated. Applying all of my firearm training I squeezed of one shot. BANG! (A .45 caliber pistol makes a loud noise.) Nothing happened, it was a clean miss. I had just launched a bullet in a northwesterly direction across the most densely populated area of the county! I nearly panicked but I had no time to worry yet because the cat was still there. I fired again this time aiming at its chest. The cat then leapt out of the tree and knocked me over. Did I miss again? Am I shooting blanks? The animal was not trying to get me, but it had a good reason to do so. Foolishly I had left it no other escape route. This time I did have a very real moment of panic. I now had possible injured cougar running toward a kids T-Ball game! (19) Much to my relief I found the cat stone dead, about 100 feet away. I loaded it up, left the area and informed my chain of command.

I received nothing but support from my supervisors and local police. Not so with local "Greeners", who's letters to the editor alleged wildlife officers were trophy hunting inside city limits. "There's a special place in hell waiting for Officer Haw" one said. I dreaded the inevitable newspaper story especially the part about launching a bullet towards Olympia's Farmers Market.

When the story came out I was worried. However, to my amazement, witnesses reported that "the officer shot the leaping cougar through the heart out of midair while it leapt at him...it died at the officer's feet." There was no mention of two gun-shots. I did not feel compelled to request a retraction. (20)

(19) This cat has been mounted and is currently on display in the Natural Resources Building about ten blocks away from the kill site.

(20) I use this story when training new officers about the unreliability of eye witness testimony.

**

After the dust settled from the Olympia cougar incident I was contacted by another neighbor. This one told me that her husband had seen and photographed yet another cougar on the same block. It was not uncommon that cougars, particularly sub adult and breeding pairs, to run together, albeit for short periods. And quite frankly cougars in the city limits didn't surprise me anymore. I drove to their home and looked at the photo. It was 4x4 inch shot of a very blurry maple tree completely engulfed in parasitic ivy. The husband pointed out a smudge in the center of the picture that he claimed was a "puma." The man only spoke Spanish and using the wife as an interpreter he insisted that the smudge was a cougar. I had to admit that the smudge may look a little like a cat's face. I took the picture and made halfhearted plans to have it enhanced.

One could only see a cougar in the picture if they looked at it like one of those intriguing pieces of artwork where an Indian spirit is hiding behind random trees. (21)

My partner and I took the picture and magnified it. There it was, unmistakably, an image of a cougars face right in the center!

I returned to the couple and asked some clarifying questions. I ruled out that the picture was taken prior to my removal of the first cat. There was

74

definitely a second! I learned that this man, a former member of a South American drug eradication team, had survived a "puma" attack in a remote tropical jungle. (22) He showed me obvious healed scars from the incident.

This cat never reappeared but to this day it is rumored to eat miss-behaving children in a vacant lot at 11th Ave and McCormick Street.

(21) This kind of artwork is popular with wildlife officers. It conforms to their romantic image of themselves.

(22) "Puma" is a Central American term for Puma concolor, a cougar.

***

Problem wildlife work was never-ending. Almost all of these calls could be resolved over the phone if people followed simple advice. I can boil it down to about six one liners.

- If you don't want a bear in the yard, get rid of the bird feeders.

- A fence will keep the coyotes out of the chicken coop.
- If you don't want deer eating your flowers don't plant any.
- Bring the pet food inside at night.
- It's not the tax payer's burden to buy you a fence.
- Secure your garbage cans.

Instead, the State of Washington choses to pay highly trained police officers $45 per hour to drive out and say this in person.

***

Once in a while problem wildlife work threw me a curve. I received a call from a distraught woman with a bat in her home. I hate bats, they scare me. The woman explained to me that her two year old may have been exposed to the animal. She was upset because the Olympia Police Department would not respond. (I don't blame them.) Reluctantly I drove to the large older home only a few blocks south of the Governor's Mansion in Olympia. I recalled a fairly recent story where a Lewis County kid had been exposed to rabies and died under similar circumstances. Hiding my aversion to bats I inspected the home and soon discovered one flying from room to room. Soon enough it landed near a stereo that had a slotted rack for storing cassette tapes. The bat went inside it and assumed a position much like that of the numerous tapes. Great! I thought, I would simply trap the bat inside. While doing so I remembered that the child may have had an exposure to the animal. I seemed to recall that animals suspected to be rabid needed to be tested and that brain tissue was required for the test. (I had read this in a magazine at a dentist's office.) I realized that I needed to kill the bat without damaging the brain. Using a knitting needle that I had spotted, I leaned toward the trapped bat and plunged it into its chest. My face was so close to the opening that the bat, as it was being pierced, hissed and exhaled sharply in my face. I clearly felt a hot mist hit my nostrils and eyes. I recall thinking, what's the chance of getting rabies? Well, none if I get 12 one foot needle injections into my stomach! (I believed that "twelve in the belly" was the conventional treatment for rabies at the time.) What are the chances? I carefully cleaned up the area and the needle with bleach and bagged up the bat. The woman was very appreciative. She later sent me a beautiful thank you card that I still have. I drove directly to the County Health Department and dropped off the bat for testing. I really did not worry at this point. After all you have to get bitten to get rabies anyhow. I'm glad I included my personal phone number.

Later that same day I reluctantly checked the messages on my old style answering machine. (I was ducking several girlfriends at the time so it could have been days before I did so.) The message said "The bat has rabies, see your physician ASAP if you've had an exposure." Exposure!!! Hell, I ate some of it! I drove directly to Group Health, a place that my mother calls Group Death, and spoke with a doctor. He told me that ordinarily he would not be concerned but he had recently read something in a medical journal where a group of spelunkers had all contracted rabies and died due to an airborne exposure to infected bat guano. An experiment was conducted placing a kenneled dog in the same cave.

It also became infected and died. The first documented airborne transmission of the always fatal disease was recorded. "No problem" the doctor said, "We have about 10 days to get you the antidote. The problem is it costs a lot of money and we have to have it brought out by courier from the east coast somewhere." I asked, "Is it true that I'm gonna get twelve in the belly with a foot long needle?" He laughed nervously, but did not answer my question.

I waited not without a little anxiety for about 9 days. In the mean time I watched a re-run of the old western series Bonanza. In this episode a man who had been bitten by a mad dog was chained inside a barn as a precaution. Of course he contracted rabies, tried to bite all the Cartwrights and died. I was born a little paranoid.

When finally called back to the doctor's office I received numerous shots, most of them while standing with my pants dropped. The sheer volume of the fluid injected into me was uncomfortable. I remember looking over my shoulder and seeing clear fluid squirting out of one of the injection holes until it was patched by a nurse. The whole operation was essentially painless but I had to return for numerous weekly follow-up shots. Each time I bravely told my buddies "I'm going in for twelve more in the belly with a foot long needle!" I never told them the truth. The two-year-old also got the shots, I'm told she didn't cry at all.

Currently bats are considered a sensitive species and deserve protection as such. A team of WDFW biologists are actively studying them. Unbelievably, for a time the general public was encouraged on the agency web site to collect dead and sick bats and to deliver them to regional offices. (The bat bio's had all been inoculated.) I shared my bat experience with enforcement dispatchers and strongly advised them to tell the public not to touch bats under any circumstances. The agency web site no longer makes this request.

***

I responded to a call about a deer eating a man's sweet peas. He was very frustrated and threatened to kill the deer. I told him, "Don't do that, just pop it in the butt with a BB gun." Shortly thereafter the man called back and said that he did what he was told but the deer was now acting sick. I returned to find a two point buck, very much dead lying in the pea patch. I was convinced that this man used a .22 rifle to haze the deer and confronted him. He produced for me the weapon used, which was an air rifle that fired a .17 caliber pellet at about 650 feet per second. What can I say, I fucked up. I never provided this advice again.

Years later I was telling this story to a group of very young hunter education students and their sponsors. My lesson point was that BB guns and air rifles require the same respect and safe handling rules as firearms. One of the sponsors stood up and said "That was me!" We both had a good laugh.

***

By providing a police response to nuisance wildlife calls we have trained the public to expect a police response to them. By extension, the public also thinks that dialing 911 is appropriate, when it is not. (23) As a result other police dispatch centers and their officers have become convinced that much of what WDFW does is trivial. This is where the term Gopher Choker originated. (24)

In the Olympia area, I often received calls from people demanding that I examine suspicious piles of fecal matter. Suspecting cougar or bear scat, people unabashedly, send photos of turds to our dispatch center which are then forwarded to officers in the field. Believe it or not many believe this to be a police issue! We are expected to complete an incident report and this data is collected. Almost always, it turns out to be an exceptionally large pile of dog crap. I've examined so many that I could tell you if the dog was eating canned or dry food. Kibbles and Bits leave a distinctive and colorful pile. Many of the turds I examined were quite spectacular. Often they were human, or raccoon, less often that of a bear. After nearly four decades of doing this job I don't know what a cougar turd looks like, but it seems that many Olympia "tree huggers" see them all the time! It's as if these folks think that if they locate a cougar turd, I will be able to catch the cat. They over estimate me.

(23) Dangerous wildlife calls are different. They justify a 911 call. Simple problem bears, possums, raccoons and routine sightings do not.

(24) This fact damages the WDFW reputation as a legitimate law enforcement agency.

***

Often suspicious circumstances are posted on neighborhood on-line watch boards. A single TV news report regarding a cougar someplace else, combined with the opinion of one crank, often starts a domino effect causing people to believe that they are overrun by man- eating cats. That's when all dog tracks, piles of crap, bumps in the night and missing housecats become "proof" that a man eating cougar has taken up residence.

"It's cougar scat for sure, my friend knows a hunter and that's what he was told." This is a very common rationale. I find it funny because I have been a game warden for many years, have captured many cougars but I have never seen cougar scat! People really want to believe that a cougar is in their midst, I don't know why. I often found myself making argument as to why what they were reporting was not evidence of a cougar.

Once a well-meaning rookie wildlife officer responded to one of these crank calls. Veteran officers ignored the report because we knew the source. The rookies solution was to post an alert on the neighborhood message board. *"Warning cougar in area."* This was exactly the wrong thing to do. This officer soon transferred but till the day I retired many years later, numerous crank calls from this same neighborhood were reported. These calls were clearly sparked by the two decade old message board warning that had legitimized the original erroneous report.

***

Large tracks that appear in a garden are often reported as those of a cougar. I would asked the caller, "Do the tracks look more dog like or cat like?" The answer was always "For sure more cat like? "I need to be sure before I come out." I would say "look closely at the claw marks, are they long and skinny like a cat's claws or short and triangular like a dog's claws?" The answer would always be "long like a cat's claws...definitely." I was very careful with my use of words because it was a trick question designed to rule out a possible cougar. Cats have retractable claws, dogs don't. Therefore a cougar walking through a garden would not leave behind prints displaying extended claws at all. The existence of claw marks proves it's not a cougar. When I would explain to the caller my reasoning for making this inquiry and my deduction, they would often become argumentative and then report that the tracks did not have claws after all. Clearly they wanted the prints to be those of a cougar! But the calls would stop. This scenario played itself out a hundred times over the years and I was able to rule out many reports of cougars in this way. Interestingly, I was never able to confirm one in this way.

I feel compelled to point out that not long ago there was a confirmed fatal cougar attack on a human in Western Washington. A second person was also injured in what was a very horrible and tragic event. I need to point out that the offending cat, was NOT a habituated, urban cougar but a hungry wild animal trying to make a living. Since that incident I no longer tell folks that cougars don't pose a threat to humans. However, I encourage concerned citizens to calculate the odds of such an event happening, and to compare this extremely slight risk to the many <u>real</u> risks assumed in everyday life. I encourage outdoor enthusiasts to apply open and concealed carry firearm laws and to have pepper spray. Good people would be better off and have peace of mind. The far more common predator, other humans, might think twice!

***

One Halloween night I received a midnight phone call from the local 911 center. An obviously frustrated dispatcher asked me to hold the line while she transferred a caller to me. A man began talking excitedly in what at first seemed to be a foreign language. I understood only a few words but it became clear to me that he was reporting some sort of life threatening experience with a wild animal. Slowly, after coming out of a deep sleep, it dawned on me that this man exhibited a severe speech impediment that was made far worse by a thick New England accent. I was forced to listen very closely and I often requested that he repeat himself. "A tig-eue is twy-ing to get in my house, It's at the doe, squatching and gwow-ing." This phrase was repeated each time I requested clarification. The man paused between words, clearly aware of his impediment, as if he was doing his best to make himself understood. I said, are you trying to say that there was a tiger trying to get in the house? He answered "A tig-eue!" (Emphasis added) Is a cougar trying to get in? "No, a tig-eue!" Since it was Halloween night I wondered to myself if the man was reporting a person in a tiger suit. If that was the case it was not clear to me why the deputies were not called out. I did not however, rule out the possibility that in fact a real cougar was present.

In an effort to make myself understood I assumed the caller's impediment and referred to the intruder as a possible "coog-eue or tig-eue." This adjustment seemed to help.

During this conversation the man said what I think was "jus a minue." He put the phone down and I heard five very loud gunshots. The man got back on the phone but I could only interoperate the excitement in his voice. Then I heard two much louder blasts. I was convinced at the time that two different guns were fired. I told the man, "Stay in the house, I'm on my way."

The county had passed this call off to me... The bastards! They must have had a good reason I thought. It crossed my mind that this may have been some sort of prank. I arrived at this very remote home about an hour later.

I drove slowly up a one lane gravel road and came to an isolated single wide trailer. I observed what appeared to be electronic sensors along my way. No one appeared to be home, all lights were off. I stayed in my truck with my windows and doors locked and unsnapped my holster. Was I walking into an ambush? I looked at the front door and observed a pattern of five bullet holes in it as well as what looked like two shotgun blasts from buckshot rounds. This must be the place I said to myself. Further inspection from this vantage point revealed a bright red smear on the door about waist high continuing down the entire length of the home. Reluctantly, I followed this smear with my spotlight, fully expecting to find a guy in a Tony the Tiger outfit piled up dead. Instead I found the bloodiest, deadest cougar I had ever seen, and I have seen a few.

I knocked on the door and conducted an interview. I was having difficulty visualizing what happened until the home owner pointed out very clear claw marks in the door. Clearly, a deranged cougar had tried to get into the house! The man showed me his snub-nosed revolver and five spent casings, as well as a twenty gauge double barreled shotgun and two spent 20 gauge 4/0 buckshot hulls. (Both guns had been reloaded.)

The man explained that he received a series of audible alerts inside his home from his state of the art surveillance system. A tone, each one of a higher frequency would sound as an intruder came up his ¼ mile driveway toward his home. He had time, he said, to prepare several weapons, expecting a human. Instead, he was surprised to see a cougar at his front door. He gave it ample opportunity to leave. It tried to get inside. That's when he called 911.

This man was a self-published author having researched case law associated with existing "Stand Your Ground" and "Self Defense" statutes. The entrance to his driveway was posted with a sign stating: *Any uninvited police activity will be considered an armed intrusion* alongside a copy of the Bill of Rights. I found this bespectacled man highly intelligent and very interesting. Clearly he was no one to mess with. He offered me a signed copy of his book. Although tempted, I did not accept the gift.

I collected the dead cat and promised to return in the morning to take a statement.

I awoke and at first believed that the previous night's adventure was a dream. The bloody cougar in my truck brought me back to reality. I took the man's statement but it did not shed any light on what was already proven by the evidence. The cat was necropsied by the department veterinarian. Brain tissue, organs and blood was sent to a laboratory. I recall looking at and collecting some of the stomach contents. The animal was an apparently healthy, 100 pound adult female.

***

I received a rather routine report of a bear in a tree. I recognized the address as being very near the new Cabela's retail outlet in Lacey, Washington only about five miles from my home. I arrived at a rather industrial area adjacent to Interstate 5 shortly thereafter. Sure enough there was a very large black bear about forty feet up a good sized fir tree. A few phone calls later I had an officer with immobilization gear on his way and my sergeant was due momentarily with a transport cage. Everything was under control.

Officer Flowers loaded up the tranquilizer gun and made a well-placed shot that had no effect. A second load was administered but still the bear did not go to sleep, then a third. Flowers mumbled something about only having the short syringes, the ones with the needles more suited for deer or cougar. We were worried that the drugs were not penetrating the thick layer of fat underneath the hide. We all three brainstormed the problem. None of us had any training other than to guess approximate doses and to use the drugs that were issued. We had no idea if the drugs would take effect later or not at all. Flowers speculated that if he could shoot a dart downward at the bear, he could hit an area with a thinner fat layer. Although more than willing to climb a tree to do so, there were no other trees in the area. This guy comes from a family of firefighters. He had no fear of heights, unlike me. He had the idea of calling out a City of Lacey Fire Department ladder truck. He said that it would be no problem to be extended out on the ladder over the bear, and that would afford him with a suitable shot. Great idea! The fire department was more than willing to help out as if there was a house cat in the tree. In no time, Flowers was strapped in and extended over the bear. He made a perfect shot. Much to my relief the bear quickly went to sleep, landed in the capture net and was safely placed inside the transport cage. My only regret at the time was that this heroic act was not captured by local news crews who usually arrive just as something is about to go wrong.

Feeling good about our efforts Sergeant Makoviney and I towed the bear away to the cheers of those who witnessed the capture. Secretly we were worried. This bear had taken several large doses of drugs and we had no idea when or even if, the bear would wake up. There are many policies in place that greatly limit our options when releasing a habituated bear even if it's not loaded with drugs. We discussed violating policy and releasing the bear on public timberlands. (25) Or, we could stay within policy by simply euthanizing the bear, but neither of us wanted to do that. We argued about what to do while towing the bear generally toward a block of public land where I thought we could release it without getting caught for violating department policy. Suddenly we received a report of a cougar at a day care center. With no other information to go on this kind of call trumps all others. We had to get rid of this bear and the cumbersome trap ASAP. The difficult decision was made for us, the animal was dispatched and left in the woods. (26)

(25) Releasing a habituated bear is not as easy as seen on T.V. Officers assume a great deal of liability and could be held responsible for the future actions of a released bear.

(26) Policy prohibits the release of a "drugged" animal during or just prior to hunting season, made more problematic by tribal seasons being potentially year round. For this reason the bear could not be donated for human consumption.

***

I have lost track of all the bears and cougars that we have caught or killed over the years. These incidents are often reported on local television news casts. I'm sure that it's interesting to the public and that viewer's feel good when a successful relocation is reported. Most wildlife officers know better. The fact is that these incidents are almost always a tragedy. First of all these animals almost never pose a real threat in the first place. If people would follow simple advice we would greatly reduce perceived conflicts, unfortunately they don't.

Given the states 6.5 million people one would expect far more conflict, in my opinion.

Land owners and administrators of public lands do not want habituated bears released on their property for obvious reasons. Transplanting bears to a national park would cause an uproar. National Forest Service, state owned and industrial timberland land is a possibility but bears are known to cause a great deal of damage to marketable timber that these organizations rely upon, not to mention the perceived threat to the general public.

What is not generally known, and almost never advertised by WDFW is that habituated animals that are relocated soon come back and reassume their backyard tendencies, die from the drugs or they are killed by real wild animals soon after relocation. It's similar to a city boy trying to survive the winter in Alaska! He simply does not have the survival skills. The same is true of urban bears and cougars. Life is easy for them until placed into the real wild, where long term survival is not expected.

There are other urban myths surrounding bears and cougars. Sadly these are often perpetrated by the Washington Department of Fish and Wildlife. One being that human activity is currently displacing large carnivores and that humans are causing the conflict. While partially true there is far more to this issue. Most western Washington cities have been well established for many years. Let's take Olympia for example. The downtown area was well established by the 1870's. It quickly grew and expanded in size. Although old Olympia no doubt had the occasionally problem bear, I'm sure that any marauding animal would have been quickly dispatched. The meat would have been consumed and the lard would have been used to make the finest blackberry pie crust on earth. (Not a problem at all but a perk.) Very soon there would be no bears. Clearly, this early local extinction was in fact caused by human encroachment. That was generally the case until the 1990's when bear and cougar conflicts took an alarming upswing. In the spring of 2019 WDFW dispatch took 36 bear complaints before 8 A.M. one morning. My crew and I quickly caught four of these bears and identified at least eight others all in S.W. Olympia. A pregnant cougar was captured in Seattle's Discovery Park, another recently swam out to Bainbridge Island!

The current issue with wolves in Eastern Washington is another example. Completely absent for the better part of a hundred years "Insurgent" wolves, intentionally re-introduced into the Yellowstone area, are rapidly expanding westward, attracted by human made food sources.

Currently bears and to some extent cougars are joining long established coyotes by re-populating urban areas due to a multitude of factors. Neighborhoods are a smorgasbord of bird feeders pet food, fruit trees, compost piles and garbage cans. Hobby farmers raise chickens, rabbits and pigmy goats. Many folks have lamas and alpaca. (Cougar's favorite food) All cities take great pride in their parks and green belts. Feral cats, non-native possums and rabbits all flourish attracting predators. People in general, intentionally and by accident attract wildlife of all sorts. These factors are augmented by an alarming drop in the numbers of folks that hunt big game in surrounding areas. We have created a habitat that is actively attracting large carnivores and they too are now urbanized. Cougar and bear occurring in cities are there by choice, it's simply an easier place to make a living. This easy living encourages the survival of less fit individuals. It's all part of a very natural, albeit manmade process. We need to accept it.

***

While driving to the office one day I observed a ruckus at one of the city's covered bus sheds. A man was out of control, yelling and screaming obscenities. He began kicking and punching the clear plastic panels of the shed. He broke several but apparently not satisfied with his work he picked up a large rock and broke even more. Where's a cop when you need one, I thought.

I approached the man and quickly placed him in cuffs. He was rational and apologized for his actions. "I'll never do it again" he said. I called out an Olympia P.D. unit and turned the guy over. One of the cops said that this kind of thing happens all the time with the homeless people and that the panels only cost $40 each to replace and the city just accepts the cost. This cop was going to let this guy go! I said "No wonder they do it! I live in this city and I'm NOT willing to accept the cost...never mind, I'll book him myself." Shamed by what was clearly a City of Olympia policy decision, the cop decided to buck the system and processed the arrest. I realized later that the cost of booking, housing and feeding the suspect would be added to the cost of the damage. Yes, the city and the taxpayers would have to eat the cost. Why wouldn't they just look the other way with heroin, hand out free syringes, let them camp on the sidewalk and legalize marijuana? That's right come to think of it, they already did that.

I needed to stick to wildlife work.

***

Some years ago I heard a state trooper on the radio sign out with a car accident on the C-4000 Line in the Capitol Forest. A short time later this trooper reported that he was enroute to the jail with a man under arrest for "felon in possession of a firearm." I was bored stiff at the time and wanted something to do. I called the trooper and asked, "Was this guy up in the forest bear hunting?" "Sure was, how did you know?

"I didn't know, I just thought it was a possibility because today was the opening day of bear season and that bears are often hunted in the Capitol Forest."

On a hunch I asked if I could meet him at the jail and interview his prisoner. "Sure, it's up to him if he wants to talk."

I soon arrived at the jail and secured an interview room. I introduced myself to the suspect. My only bit of suspicion at this point involved the fact that this man was bear hunting and that he was a convicted felon who had little respect for the law. I felt that because he was predisposed to criminal behavior, that he may be unlawfully hunting bear over bait too. I had nothing better to do.

I introduced myself to the man. I caught a very slight odor of vanilla. It's not unlawful to smell like vanilla but one would expect this guy to smell much worse based on his appearance. Also, any wildlife officer knows that vanilla extract is a common bear baiting ingredient. I asked this man to tell me about his bear bait on the C-4000 line. (The general area where he crashed.) I was unaware of any such bait station but he did not know that. He calmly denied baiting bears but acknowledged that he knew that such hunting was a crime. The trooper, no doubt thought I had some real information regarding a bear bait, but I didn't, I was just playing a hunch. I said, "I'm not here by accident, can you think of a reason why the game warden would want to talk to you?" "What would you say if I told you that your fingerprints were on the packaging materials at the bear bait site?" (This was an absurd allegation for me to make because this man's prints, although on file, had not yet been cross checked.)

"I don't think my prints are on any bait" the suspect said.

"You don't think? Why can't you say for sure?"

"Trooper Johnson, are your prints on the bait?"

Playing along beautifully he said, "I can say for sure my prints are not on any bear bait…anywhere."

"Good answer, I can also swear that my prints are not on any bear bait, why is it that this guy can't say that?"

This suspect was not the sharpest pencil in the drawer. He thought for a minute and said, "I was at the store this morning, I handled a box of pastries but I put em back. Someone else must have bought them and placed them on my bear bait."

The Trooper shook his head in disbelief. He must have thought I was the greatest interviewer ever. Quite frankly I was dumbfounded but pretended that I knew all along.

This suspect had no idea how bad he had just screwed up. He had essentially just admitted to a wildlife crime. My problem now was to actually find the bait site. An admission to a crime, or even a third party's statement leaves any investigator far short of the required probable cause to file a criminal charge. If the officer has both, he is still short on P.C. without corroborating evidence. I needed to find the bait! I asked a few clarifying questions. By now the suspect was wise to me and denied everything. My boat was starting to take on a little water.

I passed a note to the trooper. "Was anyone else with this guy when he crashed?"

"There sure was, here's his name and address."

As fast as I could drive without lights and siren I arrived at a nearby residence conveniently located just a few blocks from the jail. An 18 year old boy came to the door. "Your Uncle Jim wants you to show me your unlawful bear bait site off the C-4000."

"It's not on the C-4000, the bait is on the C-4200" he replied. Clearly these guys were related.

Together we spent a few hours observing and taking photos of well-hidden bear baits strategically placed along an old overgrown grade. This young man pointed out each one.

The suspect spent several years in prison for the firearm rap. Just before his release I checked on the status of the bear bait charge. It remained unaddressed but still active. It ultimately tacked more onto his sentence.

***

As long as I can remember fall rains have haunted me. Mature salmon, while on their spawning migration crowd river mouths, often frustrating anglers whose attempts to catch these cavorting fish go unrewarded. But when it rains magic happens. The fish seem to briefly bite the angler's offerings one last time then they disappear up their river of origin to the spawning grounds and the protection of "closed waters." Once there they are safe to spawn, or at least they should be. That's where the fish cop comes in.

Fall is very exciting time of year. Many times in my career I would awake to the sound of rain pelting down on my roof. When combined with the knowledge that fish were schooled, sleep for me was impossible. Several nights each fall, my internal alarm clock would sound. I would spring out of bed and head out, usually to where the largest concentration of fish were known to be. I was often chastised by my peers for making this decision because these impulses often seemed to conflict with planned deer decoy patrols which I found to be of very low priority.

In the Olympia area there are numerous such streams with species that all have different run times.

This phenomenon could happen the first week of September in the Nisqually River with chinook salmon and the first week of October for coho. Numerous local very small chum salmon streams are huge salmon producers too. When one considers that these streams discharge less than 1/100th of the Nisqually's overall flow, and drain relatively tiny areas, he or she should be amazed at the numbers of fish that they produce. (Sometimes more than the Nisqually.) For these small streams the magic day for chum salmon usually happens with the first big rain around Halloween.

One late October night I awoke to the sound of my rain gutters overflowing. This was it! I headed for to the lower end of Perry Creek knowing that massive numbers of chums would be moving. Poachers would be thinking the same thing. It would be a great time to set a "rag net": A disposable short section of gill net with large mesh, easily found or stolen from any local Indian reservation. Even a person with a single dip net or a heavy duty rod and reel would have no problem filling the back of a pickup with fish if so inclined.

Chum salmon roe is a hot commodity, often selling with no questions asked for upwards of $12 per pound. The fish themselves are relatively worthless and not worthy of the slight risk of getting caught. However, for an opportunistic poacher, making a quick $1000 on roe, is a very realistic goal on a night such as this.

Dressed in a jump suit and carrying two flashlights I went out. I called dispatch by phone because in these days everybody had police scanners and it was important to maintain radio silence. (With today's technology this is no longer an issue.) Within minutes I received a call back from dispatch. I was soon speaking with a woman reporting that she had confronted several persons with a gill net in Perry Creek. They had fled through the woods and no, she did not know where they were parked. I found out later that she had fired several warning shots into the air with a 9 mm pistol.

My plans were pretty much blown but I was still excited about possibly catching these guys. I was escorted to the fishing site several hundred yards down a steep slippery trail. This remote spot was tactically chosen by the poachers with the flooding stream creating a barrier between my access point and theirs. Only about five yards wide the swollen little stream would have been impossible to wade. I shined my flashlight and quickly located the point where a gill net was tied off to a tree. Potato sized floats painted black, indicating a covert gill net was extended into the stream. The poachers had clearly been interrupted prior to retrieving the net.

These guys were not coming back thanks to my well-meaning albeit aggressive reporting party. One course of action would have been for me to drive local roads looking for the pickup rig which should be possible to find but if I did, getting the suspects to admit anything would require a miracle. But the massive numbers of fish in the creek guaranteed that many fish would die if I did not disable this very lethal net. While pondering my actions I shined my light directly at it. This was a mistake that I never made again! The stream erupted in an explosion of fish. Hundreds, if not a thousand or more, panicked and rushed the net. The corks, designed to keep the net vertical in the water disappeared. The stream turned to froth as hundreds of salmon became hopelessly entangled. Unfortunately, the gill net was expertly set and functioned perfectly.

At the expense of possibly making a pinch, I spent the next several hours attempting to save as many of the fish as possible. Knowing that a male can spawn with several mates, I concentrated on saving the females. I was only marginally successful.

Despite poaching, habitat destruction, global warming, poor management, over harvest and fish cop blunders, wild chum salmon runs in South Puget Sound remain healthy to this day.

***

One month before retirement I was loafing around the office when one of our dispatchers handed me a piece of paper. It read "deer poaching in progress". I was provided with a very nearby address. Deer cases in the month of April are rare but not unheard of. This call was hot, meaning that for some reason I was confident that it was not a crank call. I raced out the door knowing that this would very likely be my last rodeo.

While enroute I received several additional snippets of information the most significant being that there was a small John Deer tractor involved. The location was a densely packed neighborhood just outside the city limits. Even though a gun was involved the Sheriff's Office did not respond because it was reported as a hunting violation instead of a man shooting up the town. Prudently, I waited about one city block shy of the address for my sergeant whom I knew was nearby. We went in together and were soon confronted by a man and wife both talking very excitedly. As is commonly the case reporting parties often start their story at the end and work their way back to the beginning, often leaving out very significant details. I heard the words "pistol, shoots all the time, drugs, dead doe and fawn, crazy, tractor."

Just as things started coming into focus my sergeant says, "There's the tractor now, and the deer's in it!" I watched as a John Deer Tractor entered the public roadway with a dead deer in the front loader. It headed down the street toward a cul de sac. I followed in my patrol truck at a speed of about two miles per hour. So rarely do I use my siren, that even after almost four decades on the job I did not even try. Instead I honked my horn. There was no response. My sergeant, who was behind me hit his air horn several times. The man on the tractor ignored us and drove through a yard almost hitting the side of a house. I was forced to exit my patrol truck and to chase the tractor on foot as it went out of sight behind the house. By the time I had rounded the corner I had drawn my pistol because I believed that the man had a gun. He was clearly in flight mode and was acting very strangely. I remember thinking that I can't die now! I just calculated my retirement benefits and my financial planner had advised me that I had to live at least sixteen years in order to get more from my retirement account than I had put in! I yelled at the man to stop and ordered him to step off the tractor. "Why? He said. I glanced at the dead deer in the bucket of the tractor and with my pistol in the "Low Ready" position I said, "Because the evidence that you are in possession of a closed season deer is overwhelming." He actually argued with me that this was so but stepped off the tractor. I placed him in handcuffs.

He denied shooting the deer of course. I repeated, that the evidence that he was in possession of a closed season deer was something I couldn't ignore! I didn't care if he shot it. It simply didn't matter as far as him being under arrest. Possession was more than enough. I gave the man an out like always. If he was frustrated by the deer eating his flowers, "I could see taking matters into your own hands" I said. As is almost always the case this prompted the suspect to admit shooting the deer at the front door of his house with a Colt .45 pistol.

He walked us through the scene of the crime, evidence and photos were collected. A Colt .45 pistol was seized. A very unique bullet was recovered from the necropsy of the animal as was a near term fetus. The dead doe was pregnant and about to give birth. The photos of the fetus were added to the case file. Trust me when I say that the suspect would not want a jury seeing these pictures. Even the most hard core poacher would be   horrified

The Urban Big Game Hunter

As stated earlier, big game animals including deer and elk are modern "insurgents" to our urban areas. Deer populations are out of control and urban elk numbers are growing. There are far more deer and elk in Washington now than when Lewis and Clark visited in 1805! This population explosion was caused by human activities. Not the least of which is logging which allows sunlight to reach the forest floor prompting rapid growth of vital food sources. Nearby forest cover creates a convenient escape route where danger can be averted. This same "edge effect" is also created in urban areas and enhanced by many species of lush grasses and ornamental plants cultivated by people for other reasons. Commercial agriculture and hobby farms create a true smorgasbord for wild animals. Many of these life giving factors did not exist before the European settlement of North America.

Currently the only big game population control mechanism available is lawful hunting. Urban hunting is problematic for many reasons, not the least of which are firearm restriction laws. Clearly not safe, the discharge of any firearm is usually unlawful. Archery hunting, although equally lethal, provides a hunting opportunity for those willing to accept certain limitations. The hunting laws do not specify how far a hunter has to be from an occupied dwelling. The use of cross bows, with recent technological advancements, and a relatively new law that allows their use, provides an additional option.

I have seen many huge buck deer and numerous trophy class bull elk harvested in such a way in populated urban areas.

Another new law makes it a wildlife crime if an animal is hunted upon or retrieved from the property of a non-consenting land owner. (Different than a conventional trespass violation.) Those that partake of this urban hunting opportunity walk a fine line, a balancing act if you will.

That said, this activity is largely not accepted by the non-hunting folks who reside here. Conflicts are common as are 911 calls. The irony being that these complainants are the same folks that howl the loudest about deer, elk and bear eating their shrubs and bird feeders.

Nevertheless, those willing to accept the potential risks, typically young hunters, often hunt for and harvest big game animals within urban areas. A practice that I encourage with not a little trepidation.

***

The Caroline Beach Country Club is a neighborhood of densely packed homes in unincorporated Thurston County. The deer are a constant nuisance for many. Aggressive does have been known to stomp small dogs and growing ornamental flowers is nearly impossible. Many local wildlife lovers will look the other way when the occasional frustrated hunter takes advantage of a sudden opportunity. Understandably a firearm restricted area, there are usually no prohibitions against shooting a bow and arrow in ones back yard. Therefor one could reasonably assume that archery hunting would be allowed by extension, provided one was properly licensed and the season was open. So, can one hunt here or not? In the absence of city or county ordinance prohibiting hunting the short answer to this question is "Yes". Hunting is lawful if one remains within the confines of his own property or that of a consenting property owner. If hunting were a violation of a local homeowner's agreement it would not be a criminal matter at all, but merely a civil issue, and not necessarily worthy of a police response. However, such hunting often generates highly emotional complaints from local citizens usually in the form of 911 calls.

***

"There's a dead deer in my yard with an arrow sticking out of it." A very common complaint in urban areas. This one I received a week before the archery season. I drove out to take a look. I arrived to a very gruesome sight. The reporting party was in tears as was her four year old child. Clearly traumatized she told me that she noticed the dead deer at about seven o'clock this morning. I examined the carcass and noted an expanding broad head and custom cut arrow sticking out of the animal. The animal was shot through both lungs causing massive hemorrhaging. These factors indicated to me that the perpetrator was an experienced bow hunter. Low velocity blood splatter clearly showed the dying animal's direction of travel. I followed this very clear blood trail in reverse. It led across the street and up to the front door of an adjacent home. Just outside the front door was a pile of apples and cucumbers splashed with blood. This was clearly a deer attractant. It was obvious to me that an occupant had shot this animal from inside the home sometime during the night, probably through an open front door. It was a simple matter to identify the home owner. A knock on the door did not produce an answer although I strongly suspected that someone was home.

The most disturbing thing was that there was a vehicle parked in the driveway with an attached sticker saying "Washington State Department of Fish and Wildlife." The government plates confirmed that it was an official vehicle. I recognized a potentially sensitive situation and immediately called my captain. I was acting sergeant at the time complete with "velcro stripes" and felt compelled to do so. (27) The boss was quickly able to determine who the vehicle was issued to, and we confirmed that the name was the same as the known homeowner. Yes, he was an agency employee.

Looking for any reason to get out of the office, my captain drove out and accompanied me for the inevitable door knock. A much disheveled man came to the door. (Hung over it turns out.) He was very polite and expressed surprise that any such thing could have happened. Suspiciously, he never asked why two uniformed game wardens were knocking on his door in the first place. Instead he made small talk. I must admit he expressed no nervousness at our presence. This guy had experience.

I knew by this time that the man had a rather extensive game violation history and was a convicted felon. He freely admitted that he was a bow hunter and in fact was preparing for a hunting trip the following week. He tried to distract me by saying that he knew me very well. A very odd claim to make, but I acknowledged that I may have met him once or twice. I then asked to see his bow at which time he said that only this morning he had taken it in for repairs. "How about arrows" I asked. (Hoping to match lot numbers or their custom cut length with the arrow stuck in the deer.) "I don't have any arrows" he said. This answer was a little too convenient for me.

I told the man "I happen to know that your bow does not need repairs and works just fine. Don't you think it's odd that two wildlife officers would knock on your door? Don't you think that we have a good reason to do so?" "Look", I said, "We already know what the truthful answers to our questions should be. Don't you think we have a witness? You are wasting our time. Ill apply for a search warrant if I have to, but either way I'm gonna take a look at your bow. By the way, how long have you worked for the Department?" Overwhelmed by this barrage of questions, the suspect, now very flustered, answered the last question only. "Ten years!" He then blurted out "I could lose my job for this." I thought to myself, you sure should!

Ultimately this man provided a written admission to shooting the buck. He explained that he had made a bad decision while drinking. I recall being told that his later version of events denied any culpability and that I had coerced the confession. (What else could he say?) That was an easy allegation to beat, my boss was with me!

This case never made the local news, I don't know why, it must have been a busy news day. I'm sure that WDFW brass was happy about that.

(27) Velcro stripes are slang for a temporary promotion. They come off as fast as they go on. I was promoted to "Acting sergeant" twice late in my career. I considered it a great honor. Although none remain that remember it, I had a brevet promotion to sergeant back in about 1990.

***

Just west of the Olympia city limits there is a marine marsh bisected by four lane US Highway 101. Some years ago a local artist had erected several large iron statues depicting a family of cattle, one of which is locally referred to as "The Mud Bay Bull." Known to many local hunters, a small herd of "insurgent" elk had taken up residence here. For several years they did not draw much attention but I did hear rumors about bow hunters sneaking in to take advantage of an either sex season. Over time several of the bull elk got large. One especially big bull elk was sometimes seen by commuters. The "Real Mud Bay Bull" was a monster. Enough to tempt almost any trophy hunter.

On the opening day of the 2017 modern firearm elk season I took a credible report of shots fired and this big bull being killed. Not only was this a firearm restricted area, the land was owned by the Capitol Land Trust and access for hunting was prohibited. It was a simple matter to find the dead elk and the two hunters hiding nearby.

Both father and son, admitted that they had killed this bull and in fact showed me a film clip of it being shot. (An interesting strategy that backfired at trial.) They said that they had permission from the landowner to hunt here. The obvious question's for me to ask was "Who? When?"

"About 15 years ago and I can't remember the guy's name."

I said, "That would make you 12 years old at the time, Where's your car?"

"We were dropped off."

"Where do you live?"

"About a mile up the road."

These guys clearly thought they knew the law and believed they had their bases covered. Getting "dropped off" made sense only if one did not want attention drawn to their unlawfully parked car. Being a Saturday, I could not reach the land owners. I would not have the required probable cause for an arrest or a seizure of the animal until I made contact with, and had a complaint from the landowner. I swallowed my pride and left after taking photos of the scene. The perpetrators, who I vaguely knew, no doubt thought they had me beat. They were grinning ear to ear when I left.

The following Monday the Director of the Land Trust provided a written complaint. I now had probable cause to make a seizure but I did not know where the meat from the thousand pound monster was being stored. Instead I inspected a local taxidermy shop and easily located the huge rack. Covering all of my legal bases I applied for and served a search warrant for the shop and recovered the antlers.

The defense argued that since they had filmed the kill, and shared the footage with the investigating officer, that it was proof that the area was open to hunting. A risky and I think stupid trial tactic, seeing as how the actual footage was not presented at trial.

Because it was the defense that brought it up, I was able to describe what I saw on the tape to the jury. Part of my testimony included my description of the film showing the death struggles of the animal which were quite graphic. At one point I looked at the jury box and saw two jurors crying.

One pled guilty, the other was convicted in a jury trial in Thurston County District Court. The huge rack was donated to the Capitol Land Trust and is currently displayed as "The Real Mud Bay Bull."

In the interest of fundamental fairness to the defendants, I must point out that if a lawful weapon was used (it wasn't) and if they had permission from all land owners involved, (they didn't) this hunt would have been lawful. Hell, I probably would have helped them pack it out!

***

About twenty years ago a story circulated about a bow hunter shooting down a helicopter with a broad head tipped hunting arrow. Widely believed, various descriptions of this incident were repeated and embellished liberally over the years. I told the story myself a few times, sticking to details as I heard them.

Recently, I was at a working breakfast associated with my new part time retirement job. Of course the B.S.

was getting a little thick and being one of two retired Game Wardens present I was under a little pressure to tell a story or two. I had plenty to choose from because many were fresh in my mind from recently writing my memoirs. I mentioned a helicopter story and was immediately interrupted by a member of my audience. Amazingly, this man told me about getting shot down by an arrow while flying in a helicopter!

"That was you?" I said incredulously!

"Sure was."

I explained that I had told that story for 20 years. It always drew great interest from my Hunter Education groups. I was never certain whether or not I told the story accurately, or if it was simply local lore. To me the story made a teaching point. It didn't matter if it were true or not. "OK, what really happened?"

This man is a timberland professional and has worked in the woods all of his life. Part of his duties involve chartering state and privately owned helicopters. They are used to conduct surveys, spraying operations and a variety of other timberland related activities. He said that in about 1999 he was conducting a survey in Cowlitz County. While flying just above treetop level he observed a camp with at least two persons. He looked again to see both wielding compound bows. Soon both were at full draw with arrows knocked and aiming directly at the chopper. One of them, he could clearly see his face, let loose an arrow. He felt the impact of the arrow on what he believed to be the rotor blades. Unsure of any damage the chopper was landed and inspected. The unit had definitely been hit but not seriously damaged.

There was not a doubt in his mind that the act was intentional although the victim could only speculate as to why. My guess, having interviewed many hunters is that they very much dislike having the game that they are pursuing disturbed in any way. Particularly archery hunters, whose assumed task is to stalk an animal to within the limited range of an arrow. Many times, bow hunters in areas where helicopters are being used have bitterly complained about their activities. They claim that the culprits are Department of Fish and Wildlife employees intentionally trying to interfere in their hunt! I've even heard the allegation that F&W Officers in the helicopters are actually spotting the elk for themselves, so they can come back and hunt the animals on their days off. I once received a formal complaint where it was I piloting the chopper!   (Again my skills were greatly overestimated.)

This common perception is fed by a hunting regulation that prohibits a person from hunting on the same day as he flies, with the exception of commercial flights.

Regardless I believe that that in this case, in a moment of extrema anger, the man merely demonstrated a momentary impulse control problem. Unfortunately this kind of reaction is all too common for adrenalin filled hunters but usually manifests itself in ways far less dangerous to people.

A criminal charge of attempted murder was considered. A charge of first degree reckless endangerment was the reported result.

The Field Training Officer

Having not had the benefit of a Field Training Officer, my professional development was delayed by many years. Simple things not taught at the Academy I learned by trial and error. For instance, operating emergency lights, using the phonetic alphabet, how the courts worked and virtually all of the knowledge that a police officer must have, came very slowly to me due to a lack of training. I am both amazed and thankful that I survived and did not get myself fired somewhere along the way. I really needed help!

In the mid 1990's WDFW Enforcement finally recognized the importance of training new officers before they sent them out to work. Sure, we were certified police officers and knew basic procedures but little else. The agency demanded additional training after recognizing the very real risk of vicarious agency liability. Also, it was simply not safe to send new officers into the field without real life field training.

I figured I was very qualified to be a FTO because I had made nearly every mistake there was and had learned things the hard way. Also by this time, because I was still learning, I felt I could relate to new recruits. I sought out and received formal FTO Certification.

My first field training assignment was an easy one. The new guy was already an angler and hunter with superior general wildlife knowledge. He was a high level college athlete and well educated. Perhaps his best qualification came from growing up in a family that pushed the boundaries of fish and game regulations from time to time. (28)

I had a great time showing this guy the ropes. I learned as much from him as he from me. This assignment was a breeze, Give me another.

(28) This officer is one of many that I trained that went on to out rank me. There are numerous sergeants, three captains and at least one deputy chief in this club.

***

Over my last 20 years or so, up to and including my last day of employment with the agency I took on many student officers. One of my main motivations was an experience that I had that I am quite reluctant to write about, but the story needs telling.

While stationed in Seattle I set records by issuing about 350 citations per year. This was easy to do and I must point out that that during a typical year I issued thousands of warnings as well. We all did. After I left for the Olympia station I began hearing rumors that my replacements in Seattle were really "tearing em up" meaning they were catching a lot of bad guys. These officers were known to be a very hard working but had little or no prior fish and wildlife experience. Someone told me that they were up to around 900 tickets and the year was only half over. I figured that these guys may be better than I was, but no one was that much better! I did some research and discovered that many of the citations were related to the recreational crab fishery which is highly regulated with strict size and sex limitations. Only male Dungeness crab, over six and one quarter inches may be retained. The numbers of citations made some sense due to the many harvest restrictions and the popularity of the fishery.

The problem was, and only a person who grew up in the area or who was properly trained would know, is that there are three species of crab caught in large numbers. They of course are the Dungeness that had strict size and sex restrictions and a daily bag limit of six. (Now the limits five when open.) There are abundant rock crab with similar restrictions and then there are Pacific graceful crab which can be highly abundant and available to shore bound fishers.

To the untrained eye, Pacific graceful crab look for all the world like tiny little Dungeness, with a maximum width measurement of about four inches. They sometimes are so abundant that a typical crab trap could fill up with hundreds after only a short deployment. Highly edible they tended to draw non-English speaking groups to Seattle area piers and docks. At the time graceful crab were not regulated, meaning there was no seasonal, size, sex or bag limits associated with them. Understandably they could be easily misidentified as Dungeness by a well-meaning, but untrained officer.

I did not believe that the new guys had been properly trained and I suspected that they may be writing criminal citations to totally innocent folks due to "new guy" enthusiasm, absent supervision and a lack of training. My chain of command ignored me when I articulated my concerns so I brought my suspicions to the attention of our in-house council. A biologist, prior to going to law school, he agreed that officer misidentification was likely. Together we created crab identification guides and sent them out to the field. The number of crab citations suddenly and drastically dropped to well below normal levels.

***

Similar stories of species misidentification by officers have circulated over the years. These incidents usually involve mistaking chinook with some other species of salmon or confusing smallmouth with largemouth bass. Few east side officers could function without remedial training on a marine boat patrol and many west siders would have trouble identifying some game fish in Eastern Washington. The potential for other species misidentifications remains huge.

Recently a veteran officer sent me a picture of a fish that he could not identify. "It's either a grass carp or a walleye", he said. These two fish species are in totally separate taxonomic orders and in no way resemble one another. The fish in question was a very common northern pike minnow! Of these three species of fish one has very specific size and bag limits, one can't be harvested lawfully at all and the other has no retention or size limit and even a $4 bounty on it in the Lower Columbia River! I find it unacceptable that an officer in the field enforcing fishing regulations would not be able to tell them apart. It happens far more often than one would think. The good news is that this officer, and many others, are very aware of their shortcomings with fish identification and they often sent me pictures of fish that they couldn't identify. Pictures of many obscure and uncommon species were sent to me over the years. I was never stumped.

Recreational fishers are required by law to be able to identify many species, some even prior to being brought to hand! Duck hunters are held accountable for identifying many species while on the wing at a distance. A deer or elk hunter is often expected to make a shoot don't decision based on a one inch antler point and very similar species at a distance of several hundred yards. The regulations demand this under the penalty of incarceration, fines, property seizure or all of the above. Clearly a fish and wildlife officer's ability to identify individual species must exceed that of hunters and anglers. (I am not proficient at duck identification. A fact that I was able to hide for 34 years.)

It was not until about 2010 that new officers received any real fish identification training. A curriculum that I created. This training consisted of a power point presentation and a very short field exercise only. It is far from adequate. Field training fails to even come close to providing the species knowledge that new officers must have. Strangely enough, some FTO's believe that training regarding traffic enforcement is more important that conducting training in wildlife identification!

Many times I brought these training concerns to the attention of higher ups. The currant enforcement administration is aware of these shortcomings and under new leadership is currently improving all aspects of field training.

***

Another memorable training assignment involved a very talented young man. He was another of those born to be a wildlife officer. Field training was a twelve week process divided into three phases. (The current process involves four phases.) The student officer receives a report card each day where dozens of training categories are rated. Phase one involves general orientation, equipment familiarity and the student officer is introduced to patrol procedures. In phase two he/she assumes an increasingly more active role in enforcement contacts. If successful the student officer moves on to the final phase. At this point the student officer is expected to make all decisions. The Field Training Officer takes no action what so ever unless safety is compromised or the student violates someone's civil rights.

On the first day of his final training phase, my student officer chose to conduct routine compliance inspections at a popular fishing area. He contacts a father and son. From a distance of about fifty feet I watch closely, making note of his positioning, demeanor, and many other things that I needed to document. I can't hear what is being said but I saw the father assume a disappointed look after my student officer inspected his gear and license. It was pretty obvious that I was going to watch my student issue this man a citation. I settled back to watch.

I was surprised when my student broke off the contact and walked towards me. He knew that I was not going to intervene unless he was screwing up. He knew the rules. He says to me "I have a question." "No you don't Jason, I'm not here. You don't get any more questions, you're on your own. Whatever it is, deal with it!" I hated to be so mean but it was his time to "shit or get off the pot." His face displayed clear frustration, a giant question mark formed on his forehead. I could not imagine what the problem was, the violator was not being difficult, Jason was doing everything right. He had written many citations under my supervision but this time I could tell that he was dragging his feet. We were going to have a talk when this was over.

He finished up the contact and issued a citation to the man. I asked Jason, "What was so damned important that you had to break off the contact to ask me a question?" He said that the man was a local county deputy and he wanted to ask me if he should write him a ticket or not. "Why the hell didn't you tell me?" I was mortified but had to laugh. I had inadvertently placed Jason between a rock and a hard place. If it were me, I probably would have not issued the deputy a ticket for this minor violation. Is that right or is it fair to others? No! But I can live with it. Jason and I had never had the "talk". Call it the facts of life or the unofficial one about professional courtesy. Bluntly stated the one where you decide in advance not to write brother cops tickets for minor things.

I contacted this cop later. I explained that we were in the final phase of training when this contact occurred and that he had placed me in a difficult situation. He too was an FTO and understood completely. He apologized. The moral of the story is that yes, a certain amount of professional courtesy is to be expected but that the real violation is placing a brother officer in a position of having to make this difficult decision in the first place! It's not necessarily in the violation itself.(29)

(29) Over the years I have cited several police officers because they crossed this line of professional courtesy. I have been stopped several

times, never for speed but at least twice with expired trailer tabs. I recently got a parking ticket.

***

One day in February, early in a training phase I was patrolling a section of the Nisqually River with a student officer. It was a slow time of year so I was trying to come up with some activity. While driving a remote access road along the river I saw something that I had never seen before or since. A very large naked man was strolling through the woods apparently without a care in the world. This guy was huge, six foot nine, 400 pounds. (In the right light I may have become a Sasquatch believer.) The temperature was in the 40's and there was a slight drizzle. This man must me suffering from some sort of mental illness and needed my help. My student officer was only about 5 foot 5 inches and quite frankly I did not have any confidence in his abilities. (30) I decided to handle this myself. The man was not doing anything unlawful other than he would have had to cross posted private property to get here. I stepped out of my truck and greeted him in the most calm and friendly way possible. I said that it appeared that he may be cold and asked if I could help. He stated. "I'm not cold." Quite frankly I saw no sign of "shrinkage". This guy was a beast of a man. My student officer laughed out loud. I saw nothing funny at the time, this man needed help. I made a note to myself to address the inappropriate laughter later. Again I addressed the man and made some routine inquiries about where he was going and where he came from. He responded appropriately. I suggested that he put on some clothes and warm up in my transport cage. He said "OK", and walked to a nearby tree where his clothing was stashed. As be bent over to pick up his pants we were exposed to a double eclipse of the setting winter sun that I swear cast a shadow on my patrol truck! Again my student officer laughed out loud. I just about slapped him. This guy was big enough to eat him in two bites and to use my leg bone to pick his teeth. In my experience nothing will make a man fight sooner than being humiliated. This guy was clearly mental and we had not even identified him yet or even determined if he had violent tendencies.

I asked the man to show me his identification. He complied and I soon learned that he had outstanding warrants for violent assaults. Now I had to take him into custody! In a whisper I warned my student officer that if he laughed again I would arrest him! (I was very angry with him but stifled it for the time being.) I practically begged this man to place his hands behind his back. He did so and I had to link three pairs of hand cuffs to do the job. The drive to a mental health professional was uneventful.

(30) This student officer did not pass field training.

***

New officers are often lacking experiences as hunters or anglers. Proper enforcement perspective is difficult to teach because only this experiences provides it. It's very difficult for many new officers to recognize what is important and what is not. This fact of life is aggravated by the fact that many published regulations are ambiguous, and sometimes total falsehoods. Many fish and wildlife rules make no sense and are unenforceable. *(31)*

Unless a student officer is already an accomplished fisher or hunter (few are), this creates a huge learning curve that sometimes cannot be overcome.

One thing difficult for many people to understand is that local discerning angler's judge the desirability of a salmon or steelhead not only by size, but by relative condition. A small "chromer" is far better than a large "boot." In other words a fish in a silver bright ocean condition is more desirable, and its flesh retains all of the fats and flavor that make salmon and steelhead great to eat. As it approaches maturity its condition degrades, fat reserves are depleted and the color darkens drastically. The fish's condition, in relation to those around it is a far higher consideration than size when it comes down to the angler's decision to retain the fish, discarding it or even going fishing at all. So important is a fish's condition to an angler that trophy sized "moss backs" are discarded by anglers for the mere chance of catching a much smaller "bright" fish.

This concept is very difficult to explain to people who are not anglers. I have often taken student officers fishing just to jump start this learning process. This training tactic helps but unless they develop a passion for fishing this perspective doesn't stick.

(31) There are many examples of bad regulations printed in the current regulation pamphlet, described in a later chapter.

***

After numerous successful training assignment my confidence as an FTO was growing. I was asked to train a female officer for the first time. I had to think about it. I was very concerned about the fact that I was not disciplined with in my use of the English language. Yes, profanity was big part of my vocabulary. Being politically correct in the modern work place remains a growing concern. Who knows what could come out of my mouth if I was not carful. My other worry, like many male cops of my generation, was that I was not convinced that female officers could tolerate the rigors of the job either from a physical or emotional standpoint. I accepted the assignment hoping that my belief in fundamental fairness would override my bias. In retrospect, by acknowledging that I had any bias at all, I should have excused myself from the assignment.

On day one I met with my new twenty three year old student officer. Being in my mid-fifties at the time I quickly became aware of a massive generational difference that my field officer training did not prepare me for. When getting to know her I focused on our similarities which included a deep interest in the outdoors and sports. I felt compelled to warn her never to feel victimized by someone else's ignorance either from inside the agency or out. The only way to beat it, I explained, is to let ones actions and decisions dictate success over time. This was my way of saying that she needed to develop a thick skin. I forget my exact choice of words but I'm sure my supervisors at the time would have cringed. The trainee performed very well.

This officer, and a number of other female F&W officers that I have come to know over the years are almost without exception, equal to or better than I in nearly every skill required for this job. I no longer carry a bias against female officers largely due to this training assignment.

***

I had many field training assignments over the years, I am guessing over seventy. The majority of these remain active officers and some are retired. A very few were terminated. I found field training very rewarding and many of my former students remain close friends. As a senior FTO, I was responsible for evaluating and providing critique to other trainers. Some were my former students. That task made me far less popular.

It is difficult if not impossible to objectively evaluate much of my career. However there is one measure of success that I attained that I remain very proud of, one that never appeared on any of my annual performance evaluations. Many of my former student officers went on to out rank me

The Poacher and Social Media

Few functional adults are less competent with a computer than I. Resisting this new wave of technology with a passion for many years, I never took a keyboard class. I contented myself with hand written or hunt and peck violation reports until I was forced to get with the times. I simply had no choice. At this point in my life I only now have enough basic computer knowledge just to take and understand an introduction level computer class. I slowly became competent enough to write an electronic report and to send and receive e-mails, but setting up an on-line account of any kind remains beyond me. At the age of sixty-one I got my first personal smart phone, but I still wish for my flip phone. I need help with nearly all aspects of computer work.

That said, it became clear to me relatively recently what a treasure trove of information violators tend to post about themselves on social media. This fact is a gold mine of information for any investigator and it has been the downfall of many poachers.

People who recreationally poach fish, keep secrets. Like lawful fisherman they believe that the truth will result in fewer fish. They choose to forget that someone shared information with them. There is something in their psychological makeup that tells them to keep their mouths shut. Sure, they will take selfies and post them on line but unlawful fish are far less obvious than unlawful game due to the fact that retention laws are different from stream to stream.. To unlawful anglers, the speed in which one retains a daily limit, the number of fish killed, and the fish's relative condition are a far greater motivation than the size of a fish caught.

Big game poachers are different. They are more motivated by a deer or elk rack than body size or flesh quality. Bragging rights are very important. Any taxidermist will tell you, far more folks have a modest sized deer head mounted than anglers have a big fish stuffed. Hunters retain, usually for their life time, the antlers or horns from animals they or others have killed. Grandpa's antlers are still in the garage, if not still on the living room wall.

Many law abiding people, even non-hunters are passionate about collecting naturally shed antlers. Its human nature to keep trophies.

It's very easy for me to understand how the concept of keeping trophies began. Clearly this practice originated with aboriginal hunter-gatherer groups. It has expanded throughout human history to include collecting mementoes of war, vacations, and even bowling tournaments! Perhaps this very human obsession explains why trophies are awarded to members of a losing little league baseball team!

I have never encountered a big game poacher whose real motivation was to feed his family. Never! Plenty however, have claimed that to be the case. So many in fact, that while conducting interviews I often gave the violator an out, suggesting that providing food was their motivation. The poacher nearly always take the bait and responds, "That's why I did it... I was feeding my family!" A Robin Hood like justification would be provided intended to make them appear heroic.

Not only is their timing suspicious, a little simple math with strongly suggest otherwise. A tank of gas costs the better part of a hundred dollars. A rifle and ammunition or a bow and arrows, not to mention expensive optics, often costs $1000 or more. There is typically the additional expense of taking a few days off work and for food and lodging. The poachers vehicle is almost always customized in some expensive way. Meat processing costs, something nearly all hunters are willing pay for, is close to $1 per pound even for basic burger. It's much higher for specialty products. Even the most inexpensive mount costs several hundred dollars. License documents are also expensive. Most poachers, and hunters in general make several trips to the local sporting goods store prior to any outing. Almost without exception wild game meat, when it finally gets to the kitchen table is actually <u>far</u> more expensive than the choicest beef on earth! The expense of possibly getting pinched is almost never considered until much later.

I'm sure that there are a few poachers motivated by providing food for their family, but I never met one! Providing food is a rationalization for poaching, not a motivation. It's far less expensive to just buy food. Or if convenient just get it for free at the local food bank. It's kind of like saying "I robbed the bank because I needed the money." It may be true but it's still a crime!

Trophy poachers covet. They want to control, own and possess. Many enjoy the killing part but its holding the antlers and the recognition that they crave. They relive the kill each time they look at their mount. They are jealous when they look at someone else's larger trophy and gloat when theirs is bigger.

The trophy poacher may be wealthy, they are almost always white, and often middle aged. Getting their trophy into the record books is the ultimate goal. They take great pride in their equipment and hone their shooting and tracking skills. Conducting research regarding the animals they hunt, preseason scouting and yes, researching the local regulations and how to beat them is a priority. I have known them to consult with criminal lawyers prior to a hunting trip. They would probably even buy this book!

They may be professionals and upstanding citizens in all other aspects of life. To them, shooting a doe or small buck, even if lawful is unethical or at the very least something not worthy of their tag, They commonly seek out the company of game wardens probably as part of their research, and are often members of wildlife organizations. Often they will give their meat away to charitable organizations or to those they consider to be "needy neighbors", but they always keep the trophy antlers. They may be quick to report what they consider to be egregious violations but they can easily rationalize their own.

One thing I know for sure, no one hates a poacher like another poacher. This fact is so obvious to me that when I assist a prosecutor in the juror selection process regarding a poaching case, I strongly recommend that he seek out and accept the poacher if there is one in the jury pool.

Compulsions exhibited by big game poachers include incriminating "selfies" which are then stored in computer memory mediums or on cell phones. Most unlawful bear bait stations are set up with hidden trail cams so that poachers can monitor animal activity. When these images are analyzed a clear pic of the suspect is usually obtained.

Damning evidence of past unlawful hunts always seem to exist. When I first started law enforcement work, seizing a rifle a bullet or even strands of hair from the back of a pickup was the ultimate evidence in charging a big game case. Now it's all about the officer getting his hands on the suspect's cellphone, or their trail camera. Better yet the computer hard drive at home!

Of course all of the rules of evidence apply to electronic records, it's the same evidence game with a few twists. Search warrants, consent searches and data analysis often result. So often is evidence of wildlife crimes contained within electronic devices that only rarely is a search warrant written that does not request an analysis of electronic memory known to be under the control of the suspect.

***

I received an e mail with a picture of a trophy class buck deer that had been posted on line. The photo was not dated but the reporting party stated that this animal, killed before the opening, was well known in the area and many locals were patiently waiting for the chance to lawfully harvest him. On line commentators were very angry but stopped short of naming the suspected shooter. A local officer soon received a tip from a family member of a suspect. The case was passed off to me. I recognized the name, I knew this guy! I had known him since he was a kid and taught his hunter education class. Recently I had taught at a seminar called "Crime observation reporter training" or CORT. It's part of a process where citizens can qualify for special hunting opportunities upon successful completion of the course and a very rudimentary background check. (Wildlife violations were a disqualifier.) The suspect had taken and passed both of my classes!

The case was far from a slam dunk. The suspect could have posted a pic of another's buck.

It could have been from out of state, years old, or even a lawful archery season kill. These possibilities and many others had to be ruled out. It was a simple matter to conduct a "door knock" at the suspect's house and enquire about the big buck. If the suspect didn't want to talk, I would be out of business.

A truck, identical to the one shown in the photo was parked out front. While walking to the front door I observed deer hair and dried blood in the back. This is getting good I thought. I was greeted by the suspect as I walked across the yard. I said, "Do you remember me Dustin?" I have forgotten his exact words but it was clear that he did. My uniformed presence alone was enough to make him nervous but he turned to jelly when I called him by his first name. The presence of a second officer put him on the brink of some sort of breakdown. I saw an opportunity to take advantage of this situation. I can be quite ruthless when my gut tells me that I am on to something. Before he could talk I said "Do you remember what I taught you at your CORT class? You know, the part about the game warden always knowing the truthful answers to his questions before he knocks on a suspect's door! Do you remember that Dustin, Do you remember that?" I must admit that my being six foot five in work boots, a little on the ugly side, and employing direct eye contact, helps a little in these situations. His answer was a very sheepish "I remember." (At this instant I knew I had him.) I then showed him a binder I had created for just this purpose displaying a cover picture of his dead, closed season buck as well as the entirety of my case file to date: About 100 blank pages! (A rather underhanded but lawful trick that I employed many times.)

Numerous times in my career suspects have lost control of themselves in my presence. At least one wet himself, about a dozen threw up, several fainted, or at least pretended too, and two actually messed their pants. This guy looked like he was going to do all of the above. Instead he cried like a baby. Tears were streaming down his face and his sobbing was uncontrollable. I almost started crying too! I really felt bad and worried that I had come off a little too strongly. We had not gotten to the Miranda warnings yet but as I was reaching for the card for that purpose he started confessing to things that I did not even know about. He said, "This is the worst day of my life." He added that he had been arrested for driving under the influence last night and had to be at his arraignment in just a few hours. All his guns, including the one that he poached the buck with had been seized for safe keeping and were locked in a secure police storage facility. (They will be easy to locate I thought.) He kept going on and on and when he was about to tell me where the missing Watergate tapes and Jimmy Hoffa's body were, I stopped him to obtain a written Miranda waiver. The guy totally caved in and admitted to spotlighting the closed season buck in question, and to killing and failing to tag a second buck deer.

I asked if he had any pictures on his cell phone of the unlawful deer. I said it in a way that suggested that I knew he did. Of course he did! He begged me not to take his phone but offered up the camera's memory card instead. I showed him mercy at this point. I truly felt sorry for him. There was one more task however. I needed a consent to search his garage. He provided me with informed consent. I recovered the large trophy class buck deer that was just starting to rot. (Clearly he did not poach this animal for food.) Its head and antlers had been removed and were carefully laid out on the floor and prepared for the taxidermist. I also observed the antlers of a second unlawful kill.

I applied for a search warrant to examine the memory card. I recovered all pertinent photos that I needed to make my case. Including pictures that incriminated several other former students of mine in unrelated violations.

This young man did not learn his lesson. He was soon cited again for an egregious fishing violation and within five years was convicted of poaching another closed season buck that resulted in in a felony charge. This avid hunter / poacher is currently riding out a license suspension. We will get him again.

***

I was asked to assist Grays Harbor, Washington officers with the serving of several local search warrants. The case involved the unlawful take of numerous trophy class bull elk in Montana. Detectives drove all the way to Montesano, WA. They briefed us prior to serving the warrants which had been written by a local officer using probable cause developed in Lewis and Clark County, Montana.

The detectives explained that a group of Washingtonians had for years been hunting a private ranch near Great Falls. They all lived in the Aberdeen area. Their lawful hunting activity was limited to deer, but the investigators had turned up evidence that these guys had all illegally taken trophy class bull elk. The ranch that they were allowed to hunt was closed at the time for elk but it also was a well-established winter range. Thousands of elk, almost all adult bulls inhabited this ranch. The detectives speculated that after years of hunting late season whitetails the suspects finally gave in to temptation and each killed a trophy class bull. As long as they all kept their mouths shut, they figured that they would get away with it.

This investigation began the previous March when a professional "shed hunter" located scattered elk bones in the snow that were missing the head and antlers. After the snow melted a springtime search of the area actually turned up the miniscule paper wedges removed from an elk tag recording the date and month of the kill. A look at the ranch owner's records revealed the names of the party that had paid to access the area at the time. (These gamies were good.) This bit of information was not nearly enough to get search warrants for the shooters homes, they needed more. They started monitoring public Face Book postings of the suspects. There was nothing found related to this hunting trip. That in and of itself, was suspicious. Then a bit of luck. One of the suspect's sons posted a picture of himself proudly posing with a trophy class elk rack. The photo was taken inside some sort of metal building. Prompted by a comment from a Face Book friend it became apparent that this bull was in fact "My dad's Montana Bull."

Montana elk hunters are required to check their elk harvests at an official check station prior to leaving the state. None of this party had done so, further complicating this conspiracy. There were many other bits and pieces of information that were presented to a judge in a search warrant application and affidavit. With search warrants in hand we were ready to knock on doors.

Numerous mounted trophy elk racks were recovered. Some were proudly displayed on living room walls. What did they tell their dinner guests? Or their wives for that matter? Did they conveniently leave out the part about poaching the animals? How did they rationalize this act? When they take their evening drink and look up the head mount, do they relive the experience?

There's one reason, and one reason only that the truth was left out of their stories and perhaps their short term memory. The antlers were just so big!

Unfortunately all of the suspects became aware that the son of one of their own had sunk their ship with a Face Book selfie. Even after confessions were gained and numerous racks seized one of the shooters held out. He admitted guilt but simply could not bring himself to submit his set of antlers. He wanted them that bad! He told investigators that he had dumped the rack in the woods and he even spent most of a day leading the detectives on a true "snipe hunt", pretending to be looking for them. The investigator's diligence finally paid off. One of them later told me that in a moment of frustration he chastised the suspect, not a little. The poacher finally produced the antlers. They had been at his house the entire time. He had hid them 80 feet up, secured in the top of a fir tree! (Unless this tree fell in the officer's presence they otherwise would never have been recovered.) He cried like a baby and said goodbye to the rack as it was seized.

In this case justice was served. The moral of the story is that for far too many, antlers aren't everything, they are the only thing.

***

The great "Paddle Wacker Case" was a personal favorite of mine. I'm not sure why but perhaps it was because I shared the experience with a student officer and it opened the doors to many training points that rarely get covered during field orientation. Another reason could be is that it was one of those rare cases that was totally documented on film. An investigators pipe dream.

A reporting party had tipped off headquarters about a video clip that had been posted on Face Book. The clip was copied to a disc and handed to me. I recall one of our dispatchers showing me how to view it on my laptop. I didn't know how.

The film depicted a local Indian tribe preparing for their annual canoe journey. Wonderful dugout canoes were being paddled by young men and woman singing tribal songs. The area was immediately recognizable to me as being in my patrol district in south Puget Sound. The film focused upon a large buck deer swimming in the vicinity. Not an uncommon site, but the fact that this animal was so big and its antlers were in full velvet made it quite remarkable. Then a strange thing happened. The canoes started pursuing the animal. There were lots of shouts, identical to those heard in old western movies. The camera panned to a paddler seated forward, and showed a young man testing the edge of a buck knife. I thought to myself that this was going to be interesting. One of the crew members struck the animal with a paddle on and about its head repeatedly. Another grabbed its antlers. Prompted by the cries of those present the man preparing the buck-knife dove over the side of the boat and swam towards the deer with knife in hand. (It was clenched in his teeth at one point.) He made contact with the animal. He climbed on top of the swimming and panicked deer and stabbed it repeatedly, sometimes while under water. The surface of the water was immediately covered with a massive slick of blood. Several boats were involved with attempting to drown the animal. The shouts and stabbing continued. I admit that I was shocked and actually stopped the film because I was not prepared for the sheer violence of it all.

A snippet of this film was released and aired on the five o'clock news. It was far too graphic to show in its entirety. Of course the tribal members not present expressed outrage for the T.V. cameras while pointing out that this was not typical of a tribal hunt, but none of the many witnesses came forward. I later seized some of the meat, the knife and the truck that transported the meat. We were directed by our chain of command not to seize the canoe although we were allowed to examine it in the presence of tribal authorities.

I showed this film to one of my former student officers. In less than a second he identified the man who stabbed the deer. He had arrested him before!

What disturbed me the most about this incident, and it bothers me to this day, was that the tribal police and other tribal officials would not identify <u>any</u> of the many participants from the video except for the one man who stabbed the deer. (Coincidentally the same one that we were able to identify.) No one in my work group except for me ever questioned this fact. This suspect was the only person involved who was a member of a different tribe! He was hung out to dry.

"That", as Paul Harvey would say, "Is the rest of the

Story.

Bad Regulations

Nothing hurts more than the truth.

Nothing is funnier than the truth.

There is nothing more inflammatory than the truth.

Until the truth is brought to light an error can't be

Corrected.

One would think that a professional Fish and Wildlife Officer would be an advocate of existing recreational fishing regulations. Generally speaking I am not. Some regulations are needed for sure. Many however are unnecessary and ambiguous. I find myself constantly pointing out total falsehoods and impossible to enforce regulations that are published and distributed by the tens of thousands each year with the expectation that anglers comply. Many times while handing out copies of the regulation pamphlet the angler's response would be "Thanks for the two day supply of butt wipe." More discerning anglers would simply roll their eyes and walk away.

The agencies solution was to create a regulation app for smart phones. The problem is that it's the exact same language! Many informed field officer's laugh, or should I say, cringe about it. I once met two anglers arguing about the regulations. Both were comparing their research, one was looking at his iPhone the other at his Android. The former showed the daily limit as two salmon, the latter clearly said the limit was four. I was asked to settle the matter once and for all. I was stuck between a rock and a hard place! I had no phone at all and a two mile walk back to my truck. These very conscientious anglers were entitled to an answer now. The only thing that I could come up with was "Go with the Android." WDFW is aware of this flaw in the system but a solution was NEVER passed down to field officers. I did not know what the limit really was…still don't! Here alone lies a readymade defense to many recreational violations.

In the last several years WDFW has repeatedly acknowledged unnecessary and ambiguous regulations in published press releases. They have promised to address the many obvious problems. Their minimal efforts have failed.

Clearly, managing fish is a very complex matrix of biological, economic and political considerations. Pleasing all constituents is an impossible task. It sometime seems that managers have given up trying to please any.

Regulations pertaining to freshwater game fish and hunting are relatively easy to interpret and are fairly well written. The regulations regarding marine fish are a disaster.

Depending on the individual courts, fishing crimes are often rejected or not filed at all. Fairly well stated in the Revised Code of Washington and in the Washington Administrative Code, the laws are clear to the trained legal mind. But the legislative intent and common sense gets lost when these rules are translated into the recreational fishing pamphlet. Well-meaning fish managers that are responsible for this, many of whom do not fish are to blame. Each have their own "species of concern" but a poorly written rule that appropriately protects one, often overlaps with a rule that is not appropriate for another.

More language is added each year to fix the problem. The result being a big bowl of sour soup! Some published regulations are not merely ambiguous, they are clearly false statements. There are many examples. Here are a few:

On page four of the current fishing regulation pamphlet it is flatly stated:

*"**You May Not:** Transport live fish without a permit"*

Clearly this attempt to be unambiguous fails. The real reason for this law has to do with unauthorized introductions of fish, it's not at all a recreational fishing rule. This rule appears to say that a bass fisherman needs a special permit to keep his fish in a live well? I guess live bait on Puget Sound is out of the question. A smelt fisherman had better make sure all his catch is dead before he walks off with his bucket. A live fish stringer is also contraband as are live crab or clams in a bag. Heaven help the person leaving Pets Mart with a live goldfish!

You May Not: *Snag or attempt to snag fish.*

This well-meaning attempt to be unambiguous also fails miserably. "Snagging" is a very common and lawful way to collect live forage fish. This is yet another contradiction because one apparently can't transport live fish either! The fact is, that it is actually <u>lawful</u> to inadvertently snag salmon provided lawful gear is used, although snagged salmon are unlawful to retain if caught in fresh water. Not so in marine areas where an accidently snagged salmon or any other so hooked food fish (when open to fishing) may be retained! Clearly a person with no angling perspective, nor one with any legal knowledge, wrote this! There are many other examples:

Take a look at the definition of "angling" on page ten.

Angling (Hook & Line Fishing) *Fishing for personal use (not for sale or barter) with a line attached to a pole capable of being held in hand while landing a fish, or a hand-operated line without rod or reel.*

If one is fishing "for sale or barter", or not for "personal use" he is apparently not "angling". If so it appears that a fisher does not need a recreational fishing license! Managers will argue that if a person is fishing for sale or barter officers should simply charge a felony crime of commercial fishing without a license. Again a lack of perspective becomes apparent, this is almost never a plausible option.

Why do they use the term "rod" and later a "pole" in the same sentence? I always thought a fishing rod and fishing pole was the same thing. Now they need two more unnecessary definitions that do not appear! This definition of angling appears to suggest that angling is allowed for "personal use" only. Does that mean an angler can't share his catch? Strangely, the term "personal use" is not defined.

Regulators need to use Webster's Dictionary for definitions. This solution is <u>reasonable,</u> far less ambiguous and it's what the courts do anyway.

If these individual points seem nitpicky, the reader needs to understand that when combined with many other ambiguities, they weaken our officer's ability to enforce any regulation. (32)

Just for fun let's look at one more definition in the regulation pamphlet that apparently many WDFW managers think is useful:

Freshwater Area: *Those waters within any freshwater river, lake, stream or pond. On the bank or within 10 yards of any freshwater stream, lake or pond. On or within any boat launch, ramp, or parking facility associated with any freshwater river, lake, stream or pond.*

This nonsensical definition serves no purpose nor does it support any recreational fishing regulation that I can imagine. I can think of many "saltwater" boat ramps, literally with live marine organisms clinging to them , "associated" with a nearby river that are defined as "freshwater areas" because of this.   Clearly there is at least one manager that thought it was important to distribute 250,000 copies of this gobbledygook to the fishing public, and many others must have agreed!

Why are salmon classified as game fish in some areas and as food fish in others? Is it so a commercial fisherman won't set up operations in an inland lake that has a kokanee, chinook or coho fishery? That's the only farfetched reason that I can think of. These areas are already permanently closed to commercial harvest. Strangely enough, landlocked chinook, coho and sockeye salmon are regulated as "trout." Ambiguous?

Ask yourself, who writes this stuff?

Don't let WDFW fish managers tell you that they don't know these things, I have loudly and often, spoken and distributed all of these points and many more in writing, throughout WDFW.

Recent attempts at regulation simplification have backfired. Instead of making the regulations simpler, they focused on making corrections. Corrections require more, not less complicated language. I am convinced that managers recognize a problem, but they can't seem to understand that the solution is in simplicity. There has been no improvement. It's getting worse.

Two or more fish cops often can't arrive at the same interpretation of the regulations without an argument. I am telling you that too often, officers interpret and apply them differently.

The Department of Fish and Wildlife formally "classifies" countless organisms as "unclassified" making them unlawful to possess. Therefore, technically, you can't use a marine worm or a shore crab for bait! How else is a kid going to learn how to fish? Did you know that it's unlawful to keep a tadpole in a jar or to temporarily keep a garter snake in a box? All the things budding biologists and wildlife officers did as children are now illegal act because many managers are unaware of the repercussions of their actions. How are the next generation of biologist and officers, something we so desperately need, ever going to develop the required passion or interest in fish and wildlife? They will have to learn it on their smart phones I suppose.

Blissfully ignorant regulators fail to understand that ambiguity creates a potential affirmative defense to any prosecution. Courts <u>must</u> rule in favor of the party that did not create the ambiguity. (32) The regulators often neglect to consult with informed and experienced enforcement officers prior to making the rules. ("Experienced" means those officers with both the angling <u>and</u> the enforcement perspective.)

No one can walk on a beach at low tide and not kill thousands of marine invertebrates but if you use a sand flea for bait you can get a ticket! Unbelievably one can get arrested for picking up a sand dollar!

And at the same time agency managers can't understand why far fewer people are going fishing and buying licenses!

My biggest frustration during an otherwise very happy career has been in trying to make regulatory improvements and simplifications. Currently a person can very easily be cited even though they made every reasonable effort to fish lawfully. There are a number of WDFW employees in this club, but I doubt that any would admit it. The enforcement program is not at fault. Responsibility lies with general management.

I once caught a steelhead on bait in a bait prohibited section of a stream. I had no idea that I was a criminal until I got home. The law was ambiguous. Had this happened before I was an officer, it would have been exposed on my polygraph examination and would not have got hired. Had I been pinched, like I have done to others many times, I would have faced severe discipline and perhaps been terminated. My whole life would be different. I might have turned into a poacher.

I recently went fishing on the gulf coast of Texas. There were many species new to me and all had their own regulatory complexities. I worried myself sick making double sure I had all the correct non-resident permits. I sat down to review the regulations. I fully expected that their rules would be worse than those in Washington. This can't be right, I said. This is too easy and simple to understand. I must be missing something! I soon relaxed and enjoyed myself immensely. We could learn something from Texas.

Granted, the regulatory issues in Texas are far different than here. Out of curiosity I developed an interest with regulations published by the Province of British Columbia Canada. Their fish management issues are very similar to our own. I found this fishing regulation pamphlet very easy to navigate, far superior to that of Washington.

The writers of our regulations will argue that I am focusing on minutia. Well, I developed that habit after being sued for false arrest over writing a simple over limit case. The plaintiff's lawyer looked at the small stuff too! I went through hell for three years over a poorly written law. The writers of the regulation pamphlet and their families didn't get sued. I, and mine did.

I could go on and on regarding page four of the currant regulation pamphlet alone. There are 135 other pages in the pamphlet (2019) that require similar scrutiny. Many of the definitions on pages 10 and 11 do not occur anywhere else in the publication. Why are food and game fish defined at all, I thought the agencies merged in 1994! I will admit that specific regulations for many bodies of water must be complex in order to allow for _any_ angling opportunity, but even those are ambiguous.

Do I appear to be angry? You bet I am!

Poorly written fish and wildlife regulations greatly diminish the overall quality of outdoor recreation in Washington State. It also reduces participation and license revenues.

I have written and submitted up my chain of command every thought I have had on this subject and I have forced this conversation upon many currant high ranking fish managers and directors. Most nod their heads at the right time, many actually argue, unbelievably, that the regulations are not ambiguous! Year after year this problem remains. The current agency director and commission should be ashamed of themselves, as should be their trusted advisors. How can we expect the courts to take these laws seriously when they don't?

(32) *This is a defense in which the defendant introduces evidence which if found to be credible, will negate criminal or civil liability, even if it is proven that the defendant committed the alleged act.* _**A patent ambiguity**_

is one that appears on the face of a document or writing because uncertain or obscure language is used

My Last Rant

I have made hundreds of big game cases and issued thousands of tickets for a multitude of violations over the years. The ones that I remember most fondly were those requiring interviews where evidence was light and an admission was imperative. Some of my decisions haunt me. I became quite expert in getting a confession first, which inevitably led to corroborating evidence and a chargeable case. Many were like mini homicide investigations and some involved complicated forensics.

I collected tissue for DNA analysis, recovered bullets for ballistic comparisons and analyzed cell phones. Deleted and lost photos and damning text messages were recovered by such means. I wrote many search warrants, I'm guessing over one hundred. Far more than a regular police officer would do during an average career.

Investigation was a huge and "fun" component of the job. I have also assumed false identities and infiltrated criminal groups.

One such assignment lasted nearly four months and involved living with a female officer posing as man and wife. (That experience alone was worthy of its own book.) I set up and executed many covert buys of drugs, fish, shellfish and game meat, even live piranha's, usually while flying by the seat of my pants.

Looking back, all of these experiences were rewarding to me and lawful hunters and anglers benefited by having more game to hunt and more fish to catch. Poachers were hampered by my efforts and my mere presence created a deterrent which no doubt saved many animals.

The problem is that my patrol efforts for the most part involved animals that were not species of concern! To say it bluntly, deer, elk, big game in general, introduced pheasants, wild turkey, hatchery produced salmonids, non-native game fish, non-native clams and oysters, do not need our protection nearly as much as sensitive habitats and many other species of greater concern, mostly wild salmon. (To disagree with this statement strongly suggests a poor grasp of proper perspective.)

I realize now that much of my career was spent protecting lesser sensitive and non-native wildlife when I could have used my skills protecting the many at risk habitats and associated native species that really needed my help. It's a very long list. Big game enforcement is important but mostly from a fair chase- harvest opportunity standpoint, not necessarily one of conservation. (There are exceptions.) Again, very bluntly, if there were real conservation issues regarding deer, bear black bear or elk, why are they hunted at all?

Problem wildlife work was sometimes fun but more often not. It almost never required a law enforcement response. We did it anyway because that's what the public expects.

I should have focused far more on the public safety aspect of the black market shellfish industry where people's lives are really at risk, instead of the fun stuff involving the relocation of habituated bears while perpetrating the false message of saving human lives.

Habitat protection is largely overlooked by law enforcement and related issues are not emphasized as they should be. My enforcement priorities were clearly flawed, as are those of the current Department of Fish and Wildlife Enforcement Division.

***

Recently, I observed a dead half grown cottontail rabbit on my porch, the second of the day. As usual I thought nothing of it but instead automatically reached for a short rake that I keep at the door just for this purpose. Each day I practice a lacrosse toss sending a dead animal of some sort out into the tall grass. This time something dawned on me. The feeling was powerful. I experienced a true epiphany! Over the years I have performed this act sometimes several times a day. I thought about it and tried to remember all of the different animals that I have disposed of in this way. Let's see…Douglas tree squirrels, chipmunks, cotton tail rabbits, hummingbirds both Anna's and Rufus, mourning doves, flying squirrels, alligator lizards, two types of garter snakes, bats, vole's, wood rats, field mice, shrew's, many species of protected song birds, baby wood ducks and mallards, quail a weasel and on and on. The sheer numbers of victims overwhelmed me. I calculated the numbers in my head, assuming one kill per day over the last 39 years. (I did not count non-native invasive species.)

The bottom line is that because I provided refuge to housecats, while maintaining actively baited bird feeders, a minimum of 14,235 individuals of many species are unnaturally dead. Each animal was protected by the very same game code to which I dedicated my life. All were unnecessarily killed due to my indifference. Multiply these numbers by the number of currant cat owners who maintain bird feeders. The eco impact is massive! Think about it.

I'm not saying that its so, but one could argue that dedicating my life and taking risks to catch human poachers, was a colossal waste of time.

***

The modern fish and wildlife officer is equipped with an incredible array of work related tools. Things unimagined by those of my era until a few short years ago. Glock pistols with a 14 round capacity and up to four extra magazines on their belt. Lap top, phone, camera, video cam, GPS and voice recorders, all contained in a single unit that fits in a shirt pocket. A .22 rifle for putting down injured animals. A 12 gauge shotgun. A .223 semi auto rifle with suppressor and an unlimited number of 30 round mags. An impact weapon, pepper spray, night vision, a taser, state of the art patrol vehicles and patrol boats. Many officers are even issued portable radiation detectors designed to protect against terrorist attack from improvised nuclear devices! (33)

Extensive training and what seems like constant certification updates are required for each, including at least three days each year in physical defensive tactics and combat first aid plus a full week of mandatory in house training.

All of these factors combine to attract high quality recruits to this noble profession, including extremely talented lateral transfers from other police agencies across the country. Many of whom truly are America's finest... military veterans.

The result being that WDFW has a highly trained and well equipped group of police officers with a relatively new, but solid chain of command that I would favorably compare with the best law enforcement professionals in the country. If all were passionate about fish and wildlife, and developed the proper perspective... if they all prioritized their patrol activities in a way that best serves Washington's conservation needs... the natural world and the overall quality of life for Washingtonians could be greatly improved.

(33) Oh, what I could have accomplished in 1986 with this stuff! In my day we had a revolver, loose rounds in a pouch, one pair of cuffs and a number two pencil. I bought my own binoculars and sometimes my own gas! How was it that I ever caught anybody violating wildlife laws?

Farewell

My last act prior to retirement was to send an e-mail up my chain of command. I did so literally with my last key stroke in my last hour of employment. I believed that in this way my message would carry more weight. In it I presented my pet cat analogy and questioned traditional Game Warden / Fish Cop priorities and values. I'm not sure what I expected but I received no response. This disappointment, with little doubt is what prompted me to sit down and to write more.

I remain unsure of what my professional contribution to the world has been. I will leave that determination to others. If the reader feels that I have lost hope, he or she is mistaken. I have never been more passionate about the need for fish and wildlife enforcement.

What I know for certain is that I had a hell of a lot of fun. I would not trade careers with any human being except with maybe a big league baseball player who remained active for 39 years. I no longer envy youth because no young person will ever again get the chance to do the things that I was privileged to do. I am very thankful for that.

The good news is that as our natural resources continue in their current precipitous decline, there will always be a need for professional fish and wildlife officers. Unfortunately, with great sadness I can foresee the end of traditional hunting and fishing as we know it unless voters come to the realization that our fundamental freedoms are being threatened by uninformed liberal opinion.

Being a Fish and Wildlife Officer is no longer nearly as fun as it once was, at least for me. That era is over. I am very much in favor of police accountability but currant political trends have severely limited law enforcements effectiveness <u>and</u> compromised police officer safety. I find this odd because it's this same viewpoint that claims to be very concerned about environmental protection and the need for more ecological protection laws.

Despite the present circumstances, if I had a grandchild, and if he or she told me that they wanted to be a Fish and Wildlife Officer someday, I would be pleased.

This was truly a dream job. I will never be so lucky again.

The End

Epilogue

A wise old Fisheries Patrol Officer had a few drinks and began reminiscing upon his career. He says, "You know Greg, at some point you will get frustrated. You will begin to question and second guess the outfit and all those above you. You will become convinced that you really do know more than they ever will. Simple lessons that you learned long ago will never be understood by your superiors. You will become more of a burden to them than an asset because at some point they will become threatened by your knowledge. Be aware of this and watch for your sign. It comes to all of us at some point. When you see this sign it will be time to go." Distracted by another drink or two, this old timer never got around to telling me what my sign would look like.

Several years pass and of course my old friend dies.

In March of 2019 a slow patrol day and a fond memory compelled me to take a detour. I was drawn to a great clear-cut in the Black Hills where I knew to be a large glacial erratic sticking up out of the ground, placed there many thousands of years ago by a massive sheet of melting ice. I had once attempted to scratch my initials in it to no avail. I visited this place many times in my mind over the last four decades, but not for real. I looked and looked but couldn't find it. Ultimately I walked down an overgrown old logging spur until it ended, but I kept going. There it was, almost completely hidden by a robust stand of Douglass Fir trees long overdue for harvest...This was my sign.

165

PHOTO GALLERY

This young cougar killed several lamas over a five day period. Using dogs specially trained for the purpose, they were set loose at the location of a partially fed upon carcass. The cat was treed within minutes. Animals known to kill livestock are generally killed. Live traps also work but we did not have enough of them and they were very labor intensive.

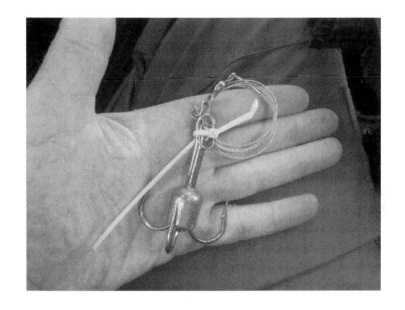

Hooks like these are used to unlawfully snag salmon. Although highly effective, conventional gear works well too. These days only a foolish snagger would use this kind of gear...but they still do.

Often during the modern firearm deer season we set up a decoy deer. It's fun work but not without hazards. A chase car hides nearby while at least one officer waits in the brush. Success is when a jack lighter shoots the decoy. More than one officer  has been forced to dive behind a log when the shooting starts. Such patrols always seemed to conflict with what I considered to be more important but less fun work, like wild salmon spawning protection. However it was important to maintain the public perception that wildlife officers were hiding behind every bush. Decoy patrols were one way to do that.

The author's backyard during deer season. Done carefully urban deer hunting can be rewarding. Ask this fella. The photo misleads the viewer. Although the setting looks wild, it was taken from my riding lawn mower. With a great deal of trepidation I encourage urban big game hunting.

    A very large cougar that lived its entire life in West Olympia. This animal would probably not have survived long if moved to the wilds. Unfortunately it was hit and killed by a car (2018). Praying largely on house cats and city deer, this is one of many cougars that have prowled Olympia streets in recent years.

An Urban Game Wardens Mailbox. "Rest in Peace Pig." I have a pretty good idea who tagged it. I wave at him every chance I get. He has no idea how much pleasure it gives me. When I was stationed in Forks, the local Gamie had his mailbox dynamited....twice! (Modern poachers are wimps.)

A successfully immobilized bear at a 7-11 store. This very young animal is typical of those that generate calls for service. It was darted while up a tree and fell into a capture tarp. This kind of operation is very routine. People feel good when an animal like this is relocated but its chances for survival in the wild is near zero.

An obvious snag injury. Even if the fish escapes the snagger, it's likely to be fatal. The wound is not the kind that occurs without a snagger's help. I have convicted snagger's by merely possessing fish with similar injuries in fresh water areas. Inadvertently snagged salmon caught in marine areas are lawful to retain. The fishing regulation pamphlet erroneously states *You May Not: Snag or attempt to snag fish.* The fact is, there are many lawful exceptions.

A "Front Yard Bull" lawfully taken on one's own property just south of Olympia. This family killed two at the same time. The other, a larger bull, is just out of view. This area is now a fully populated housing development. The elk are still there.

"Tunnel Rat Jeff" goes after a large, very angry "Injured" bear under the deck. I was much too large to get in. (Thank god) Yes, he went in and killed it with the 12 gauge loaded with 00 Buckshot. When he fired I could only see his feet!

Red Belly Piranhas offered for sale on the internet. I made an undercover purchase in a Wall Mart parking lot. A subsequent search warrant produced many actively breeding pairs. It is a felony crime to traffic in prohibited aquatic species. There is no risk of piranhas getting established in Washington waters, but juveniles could have been shipped anywhere in the country.

Another urban bear in a live trap. These animals don't need to be drugged. We just tow them away. Urban bear will probably not survive long in the real wild.

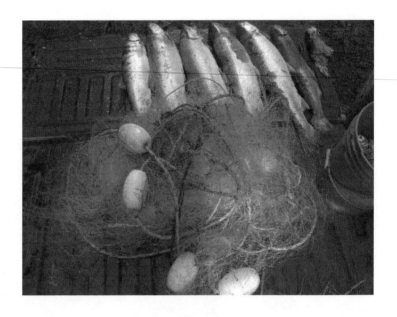

A "Rag Net" and poached Wild Steelhead from a west end river. A felony charge if you can catch the perpetrators. Officers must decide to wait for the perp to return, or to pull the net and stop the slaughter. Sometimes it's a tough call and whatever the case, guaranteed to be second guessed by know all sportsman.

A closed season urban deer kill. A blood trail, followed in reverse lead directly to the poacher's front door. Criminal charges included, closed season, no license, wastage and reckless endangerment.

A typical catch of bottom fish from Neah Bay. There are at least seven different species. Officers and anglers both have to become expert in fish identification. There are at least seven different violations represented.

The largest black bear the author has ever seen. (That's my size 14 boot in the shot.) He forgot to hibernate in the winter of 2018 and was killed by a car within the city limits of Olympia. This particular bear never generated a complaint and lived quite well. He probably had many offspring.

Wildlife officers are making an approach prior to a routine boat inspection. It's not without hazards. Officers can't pick and choose where they make their stops. This angler is far too busy to be aware of the approach of the patrol boat. A closed season "Wild" chinook was found by boarding officers.

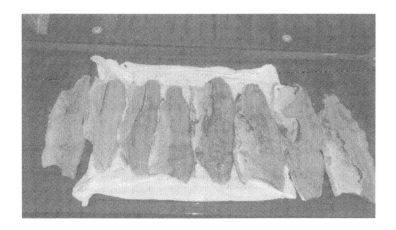

"Fillet and Release" An enterprising officer hiked into the south fork of the Hoh River. He caught two guys killing wild steelhead and releasing the filleted carcasses back into the river. A great pinch that did not get the recognition it deserved.

An urban deer hunt gone bad. A non-consenting land owner ran off the suspects. Two custom cut arrows suggested at least two shooters. The circumstances led this officer to believe that the arrows struck at very nearly the same time and the hunters were dangerously close to shooting one another. A very bad decision for many reasons.

A dead seal on an Olympia beach. The author believes that it was killed, or at least fed upon buy a six-gill shark. The WDFW marine mammal specialist insisted that the injury was caused by a coyote....What?

Black market clam harvesters digging on a contaminated beach. A high priority call for service, or at least it should be.

The Urban Game Wardens

Glossary of Terms

Anti-hunter: A person that does not consider hunting a civilized act regardless of the circumstances.

Adam Henry: Ass hole.

Beefed, to get beefed: A citizen complaint.

Bullshitter: A person who can engage his or her audience. Or a person spouting inaccurate or maliciously false information. (Not necessarily an insult) One can be a "Good" Bullshitter.

Crank: Someone who reports clearly false incidents.

Door Nock: An investigative tactic where an officer goes directly to a suspect's home. It's usually an attempt to assess information when there is insufficient evidence for a search warrant.

FTO: Field Training Officer

Glacial Erratic: A piece of rock that differs from the size and type of rock native to the area in which it rests. They are carried by **glacial** ice, often over distances of hundreds of miles.

Native Species: Flora and fauna that by natural processes belong in Washington State. Not to include those that were introduced by artificial means. **Non-native** species include but are not limited to: Rocky Mountain Elk, bass, sunfish, catfish, walleye, crappie, yellow perch, (all warm water game fish) Pacific oysters, Manilla clams, Wild turkey, and many species of game birds.

Non-hunter: Does not partake in hunting nor does he or she object to it in general.

One in a thousand asshole: The biggest asshole out of a thousand assholes. A person who blames Field Officers for all of the agencies failures and likes to write letters about it.

Pinch: A violator contact resulting in a citation. It may also mean a custodial arrest.

Ruse: A police tactic involving deception on the part of an officer. (It happens all the time.)

Redneck, Hillbilly: People in rural areas who deal with problem wildlife without calling 911. (Not an insult)

Road Pizza: Road kill.

Tree Hugger: An anti-hunter. Or a person claiming to be environmentally conscientious but still owns house cats. Usually college educated, drives a Subaru. Believes that Game Wardens have free deer neurosurgeons on speed dial and can identify fecal matter over the phone. Believes that a 50 cent / gallon gas tax will change the weather. AKA hypocrite.

Velcro Stripes: Referring to a temporary promotion to Sergeant. These insignia represent a pay raise and additional responsibilities. They may be issued or removed at a moment's notice.

WDFW: Washington Department of Fish and Wildlife.

Fishing Terms

Bank Maggot: A shore bound angler who, in the eyes of a boat angler, catches a fish that a boat angler feels entitled too.

Bi Catch: The take of a non-targeted species.

Bottom fish: Fish that tend to live at depth.

Boot Legger / Boot legging: The act of concealing unlawful fish or clams in ones boot

Brood Stock: Fish needed for breeding purposes.

Buck / Hen: Male / Female Salmon or Steelhead.

Bullhead: Small catfish or sculpins.

Bucket mouth: Bass

Bremerton Browns, Budd Bay Browns, Pukers, Turd Clams: Clams harvested from polluted beaches. (Sometimes sold in nail shops, Ma and Pa Groceries and low brow restaurants)

Corked, as in you corked me: A commercial fishing term where a fisher places his net (Floated by buoyant corks) in a place likely to intercept fish headed toward another fishers net. The meaning has expanded to cutting in line, blocking access, obstruct etc.

Cracker: An angler unlikely to catch a fish. A fisherman with hopeless angling skills.

Chromer: A highly desirable salmon or steelhead.

DuPont Spinner: An improvised explosive used to kill fish.

Egg stripper / Egging: The unlawful act of removing a salmon's roe and discarding the carcass.

ESA: Endangered species act.

Fish Cop / Creek Dick / Water Nazi / Greeny Meany / Gopher Choker / Mallard Marshal / Carp Cop / Gamie / Asshole: All synonymous with Fish and Wildlife Enforcement Officers.

Fish Hog: An angler motivated by greed.

Fillet and release: An unlawful act. Removing the flesh of an unlawful fish and discarding the telltale carcass.

Flatfish: Flounder, sole, halibut. Any fish with eyes on only one side of its head.

Flosser / Flossing: A fishing tactic where the angler attempts to appear legal when unlawfully attempting to snag a fish using lawful gear.

Forage fish: Fish used as bait. Herring, smelt, anchovy, sardines, pilchards.

Gaff: A rigid pole with a hook fixed at one end. Used to impale fish.

Ghost Net: Derelict fishing gear that continues to take fish.

Greener / Greener's: People associated with the Evergreen State College who mean well but are poorly informed regarding environmental issues.

Ground Line/ Daisy Chain: An unlawful configuration of shrimp or crab gear.

Hairy Eye Ball: The look displayed to a wildlife officer by a violator when surprised by his sudden appearance. An indication of guilt.

Hog-line: A group of boats attached to one another in a line while deploying fishing gear. An effort to retain order to an otherwise chaotic fishery.

IFD: An Improvised Fishing Device.

Indian Basher: An unreasonable person who thinks associated Supreme Court case law can be overturned by the Fish Cop. Blames Treaty Rights for their own inability to catch / kill fish or game.

Jerk: An impulsive response to a fishes bite or strike. Often an overt attempt to unlawfully snag a fish. (Not an insult)

High Liner: An uncommonly successful angler.

High Grader / High Grading: The unlawful act of discarding a less desirable fish and replacing it with a more desirable specimen.

Keeper: A fish intended to be retained.

Low Holer / High Holer : Any angler who encroaches upon another's fishing space and catches a fish, causing frustration to another angler. A reference to his relative position on the river.

Lunker: A big fish.

Minnow: Erroneously used to refer to a small fish. It also means members of the taxonomic family Cyprinidae, which are not necessarily small fish. (Carp, Pike Minnow, Dace)

Rag Net: A small disposable section of gill net used by poachers.

Sea Bass: An erroneous term for Rockfish.

Shaker: A smallish fish.

Slab: A large salmon or steelhead.

Slot Limit: A length restriction with both minimum and maximum considerations.

Snagger / Snagging: An unlawful fishing tactic where the angler intends to impale a fish on a hook without the fish biting the bait or lure. (Includes flossers.)

Snake /Mossback/ Boot: Undesirable salmon or steelhead in poor condition.

Skunked as in Getting Skunked: A failure in any outdoor pursuit.

Spawners: Love makers on a river bank or in a car nearby an access area.

Sucker: A bottom feeding fish or a person that is easy to catch / fool. Also, any member of the taxonomic family Catastomidae.

Trash Fish: An undesirable species of fish.

Two pole'er: An angler unlawfully deploying two units of fishing gear. (It is lawful to use two poles if so indorsed.)

Two Tripper: An angler aware of, yet disregards the daily limit. Hides the first limit and returns for a second.

Hunting Terms

Antlers: The hornlike growth on the head of male deer, elk or moose. Shed yearly, they regrow each spring. As opposed to "Horns" which are not shed, Goat and Sheep.

Clear Cut: A recently harvested plot of timber.

Back strapped: Describes a deer or elk with the choice cut of meat removed, the rest discarded. A poacher's calling card.

Basket Rack: A smallish, fully formed yet compact set of antlers. AKA a "brush rack."

Buck: Male deer.

Bull: Male elk.

Boar: Adult male bear.

Brush Rack: A smallish fully formed antler configuration.

Cow: Female elk / moose.

Crows Foot: An intersection on a logging road with four possible paths of travel. Resembling a crow's foot. "Take the middle toe" Meaning do not veer left or right.

Decoy Deer: An artificial deer used to tempt road hunters and jack lighters.

Deeks: Decoy's.

Doe: Female deer

Dog Hair: Thick vegetation, usually on the edge of a clear cut. "Thicker than dog hair."

Gamie: Game Warden, pre-merger.

Forked horn: Two Point. Pronounced Fork-ed Horn.

Honey Deer: A smallish buck killed by a macho male hunter that is ultimately tagged by his wife or girlfriend who was not present at the kill site. The shooters intent is to hunt for a second unlawful deer.

Jack lighter: Hunts at night with artificial light. Synonymous with Spot Lighter. (Unlawful)

Landing: A location where logging equipment was in operation. Associated with a clear cut.

LLGIMDV: Loaded long gun in motor driven vehicle.

Knife and fork rack: A one by two point antler configuration.

Non-Typical: Unusual antler configuration.

Nimrod: A hunter in the field. (Not an insult)

Old growth/ Second growth: virgin stand of timber / all other stands of timber.

Poacher: A wildlife thief.

Rack: Antlers from a deer, elk or moose. The number of points are a measure of hunter success.

Re-prod: New growth in a clear cut. Short for reproduction.

Road hunter: Drives and hunts from inside a vehicle. Shoots out the window.

Shed: A naturally shed antler from deer or elk. Easily distinguished from an antler cut off by a hunter.

Sow: Adult female bear

Spike: An angler configuration with one antler point on each side. A small buck or bull

Spur: A dead end logging road.

Spar Pole: Associated with a clear cut. Used in some types of logging operations. Often used as a hunting reference point.

Spread: A configuration of decoys used to attract ducks and geese. Also a measurement of antler width.

Sweet Spread: A deployment of decoys baited with grain. (Unlawful)

Tag Soup: A term used by a hunter who finishes his big game season without having harvested an animal. "Ill be eating tag soup this winter."

Texas Heart Shot: A non-fatal gunshot to the butt.

Tom: Adult male cougar / male turkey.

Trophy or trophy class: A legal definition. A deer or elk rack with 5 or more antler points on each side. (Not inclusive of eye guards.)

Trophy Hunter: A hunter motivated by antler size or an arbitrary measurement only.

*Dedicated to all Washington Fisheries Patrol
Officers both living and deceased. All of whom, whether
they knew it or not, had a positive impact upon my life.*

Washington Fisheries Patrol

1887---1994

Established prior to statehood

About the Author

Greg Haw began his career with the Department Fisheries in the late 1970's. He is the son of a prominent fisheries biologist and a registered nurse. Starting out as a charter boat bait boy early on, he worked in salmon hatcheries, as a port sampler, predator control specialist and fisheries technician in the then fledgling field of salmon genetic stock identification.

Always an angler he never kept a fishing secret because he was taught from a very early age that the recreational fishing opportunity belongs to the public.

Joining the Washington Fisheries Patrol Division in 1985, and later the newly formed Department of Fish and Wildlife, Greg Haw patrolled the waterways and landscapes of Washington State for 34 years. The vast majority of his time was spent enforcing fish and wildlife regulations in the relatively urban areas of Thurston, Pierce and Mason Counties, Washington.

At 61 years of age he is blessed to have his parent's right down the street and works hard at trying to apply the values and wisdom of the Greatest Generation. He feels fortunate to be surrounded by siblings, their families a loving wife and (our) beautiful daughter Melissa.

Greg remains passionate about improving recreational hunting and fishing opportunities in Washington State. Now retired he is still seeking ways to do so. Although outspoken about what he feels needs to be done, he does not have all the answers, but he knows those that do.

Acknowledgements

Those who helped me with the huge task of editing include Michael Haw, Frank Haw, and Angela Haw. Much needed technical help was provided by Melissa Morrison and Paul Denton. Special thanks go to Melissa Morrison, Jeffery Summit, Dave Spurbeck, Brian Fairbanks, James Tuggle, Emma Barns and Lauren Wendt who provided much needed encouragement and motivation. Others providing support asked not to be named but I thank them all as well, they know who they are.

Were it not for the old timers that took the risk of hiring me in the first place this project would not have happened. My heartfelt thanks are due Rowland Hatchtel, James McKillip, and Richard Kolb.

Lastly I wish to acknowledge all of the repeat wildlife violators that I have encountered through the years for greatly enriching my life and providing the material needed for this document. Only a very few were truly bad people, almost all were simply products of a hunter-gatherer culture that consider wildlife laws mere "technicalities."

I understand them more than they will ever know.

Made in the USA
Coppell, TX
08 December 2019